SUPER ST★RS

HOW THEY GOT FAMOUS

SUPER STARS

HOW THEY GOT FAMOUS

PRODUCED BY

DOWNTOWN
BOOKWORKS INC.

PRESIDENT Julie Merberg
SENIOR VICE PRESIDENT Patty Brown
EDITORIAL ASSISTANT Sara DiSalvo
SPECIAL THANKS Sarah Parvis, Claudia Atticot, Caroline Bronston

WRITER Sunny Blue
DESIGN Brian Michael Thomas/Our Hero Productions

Time
HOME ENTERTAINMENT

PUBLISHER Jim Childs
VICE PRESIDENT, BUSINESS DEVELOPMENT & STRATEGY Steven Sandonato
EXECUTIVE DIRECTOR MARKETING SERVICES Carol Pittard
EXECUTIVE DIRECTOR, RETAIL & SPECIAL SALES Tom Mifsud
EXECUTIVE PUBLISHING DIRECTOR Joy Butts
EDITORIAL DIRECTOR Stephen Koepp
DIRECTOR, BOOKAZINE DEVELOPMENT & MARKETING Laura Adam
FINANCE DIRECTOR Glenn Buonocore
ASSOCIATE PUBLISHING DIRECTOR Megan Pearlman
ASSISTANT GENERAL COUNSEL Helen Wan
ASSISTANT DIRECTOR, SPECIAL SALES Ilene Schreider
DESIGN & PREPRESS MANAGER Anne-Michelle Gallero
BRAND MANAGER, PRODUCT MARKETING Nina Fleishman
ASSOCIATE PREPRESS MANAGER Alex Voznesenskiy
ASSOCIATE PRODUCTION MANAGER Kimberly Marshall

SPECIAL THANKS Katherine Barnet, Jeremy Biloon, Stephanie Braga, Susan Chodakiewicz,
Rose Cirrincione, Jacqueline Fitzgerald, Christine Font, Jenna Goldberg, Hillary Hirsch, David
Kahn, Mona Li, Amy Mangus, Robin Micheli, Amy Migliaccio, Nina Mistry, Dave Rozzelle,
Ricardo Santiago, Adriana Tierno, Vanessa Wu

ISBN 10: 1-60320-968-9
ISBN 13: 978-1-60320-968-7

We welcome your comments and suggestions about Time Home Entertainment Books. Please
write to us at: Time Home Entertainment Books, Attention: Book Editors, P.O. Box 11016,
Des Moines, IA 50336-1016

If you would like to order any of our hardcover Collector's Edition books,
please call us at 1-800-327-6388, Monday through Friday, 7 a.m. to 8 p.m.,
or Saturday, 7 a.m. to 6 p.m., Central Time.

1 QGD 13

Contents

Rising to the Stars

Fame, fortune, fast cars, fabulous fashions—the daily lives of your favorite Superstars seem incredible, don't they? You may even dream of joining that world yourself one day—it's entirely possible. Do you have what it takes?

As you read, you will learn that the road to becoming a Superstar is not just about talent, although you do need that! You also need to be disciplined and willing to make sacrifices, and you need to know how to stay focused and push through disappointments. Most of all—you need to *believe in yourself.*

While all the Superstars profiled in this book have their unique stories of making it to the top, you may recognize some common themes: many of your faves were bullied or made fun of, in different ways, by their friends; others did not have a lot of money growing up. One thing is certain—they all were committed to reaching their goals…someday. Read on to find out *How They Got Famous!*

JUSTIN BIEBER

"I always knew Justin was gifted. Even as a 1-year-old who was barely standing, I remember him banging on tables, banging in rhythm."

— PATTIE MALLETTE, VANITY FAIR

Justin back in 2010.

HARD WORK AND SUCCESS

You may know the story of how Justin and his mom, Pattie Mallette, posted videos of Justin on YouTube—not because they wanted him to be discovered but so their family could hear him sing. But that's not the whole story of his success. He followed up the videos with a lot of disciplined effort. In his second autobiography, *Justin Bieber: Just Getting Started,* Justin writes, "Some people think hard work is—well, too hard. Me? It's all I know and a big part of the formula for success. I'd rather be working hard, doing my thing—striving to get better, to be good to people, to treat everyone with respect and work as hard as I can."

Justin and his mom, Pattie

CONNECTING THROUGH MUSIC ——

Despite the lack of material possessions in his early years, Justin lived a good life. He was close to his dad, Jeremy, even though they didn't live together. It was Jeremy who taught Justin how to play the guitar. And it was Pattie who surrounded him with music. "I'm not a musician, but music was a big part of my life, because my friends played," Pattie told *Rolling Stone.* "At home, I'd start jamming with friends, and Justin would grab a djembe [West African drum]. It was a way for both of us to connect with people."

Justin took to street performing—or busking—in front of Stratford's Avon Theatre to earn money. "I wanted to go golfing with my friends and I didn't have money, so I went out [to perform]," Justin told *People.*

NEVER SAY NEVER

Over time, music became the main thread of Justin's life. When he participated in several local singing competitions, Pattie uploaded videos of them to YouTube, along with videos of Justin singing cover songs at home, so his relatives and friends could watch them. Enter 25-year-old music manager Scott "Scooter" Braun. Scooter was searching the internet and stumbled on those homemade videos of Justin. They impressed him so much that he tracked down Pattie in Canada and placed a phone call that would change Justin's life. Scooter became Justin's manager, introduced him to R&B superstar Usher, who became his mentor, and negotiated a lucrative deal with L.A. Reid and Def Jam Recordings. And you know what happened after that! But who knows how high Justin's star would have risen if he hadn't learned the most important lessons from his mom—don't be held down by circumstances, make the most of what you have, and never say never.

LOYAL TO THE TEAM

Even though Justin Bieber is known around the world and enjoys a glitzy, superstar lifestyle, he tries to maintain a grounded attitude. He is grateful for his talent and for the people who encouraged him along the way. He is still supported by his original team—manager Scooter Braun, creative director Ryan Good, bodyguard/road manager Kenny Hamilton, and voice coach Jan Smith. He hasn't forgotten his back-home buddies such as Ryan Butler, Chaz Somers, and Christian Beadles.

Justin credits social media for contributing to his success and keeping him connected to fans. "It's something that is very good for any new artist," he told *Maclean's*. "I think that the internet is something that keeps your fans involved in the project. They can talk to you, they can write you, you're able to interact with your fans, you can keep them updated, you can put videos on YouTube saying where you are….I think a lot of older artists didn't have the chance to use the internet and Facebook [and Twitter]."

From left, Scooter Braun, Usher, and Kenny Hamilton (directly behind Justin) before a Madison Square Garden performance

BELIEVING IN HIMSELF ——————

While Justin is grateful for all his original fans, he wants to add new Beliebers to their ranks. That's what his latest album, *Believe,* is all about. The album is Justin's attempt to grow musically, a concept he feels has not been easy for people to accept. The perception that he is still just a 'tween idol' is always on his mind, but it's not holding him back. "It gives me and my fans something…to strive for next. I feel like, in some ways, I am the underdog," he told Ryan Seacrest in an NBC interview. "There are people that don't believe that I can make the transition from being a teen pop star to an adult. I just want to prove people wrong. I think *Believe* has really showcased what I'm capable of."

With *Believe* selling more than one million copies in 2012, it looks like Justin has proved his point!

JUSTIN ON GROWING UP

"There are people who try to grow up too fast—they're 18, so they're like, 'I'm not a kid anymore,'" Justin told *V.* "People need to know I'm not a kid anymore. But at the end of the day, I'm not completely grown up. I'm still learning. I'm going to grow up how I grow up. I'm not going to try to conform to what people want me to be or go out there and start partying, have people see me with alcohol. I want to do it at my own pace. But I'm never going to make myself so the kids and parents don't respect me."

CARLY RAE JEPSEN

"WHO *IS* THIS PERSON?"

Justin Bieber took on a new role for himself in 2012: music mentor to fellow Canadian singer Carly Rae Jepsen. Home for the holidays in December 2011, he was driving around with a bunch of friends when "Call Me Maybe" came on the radio. In an interview with Ryan Seacrest on NBC's *Rock Center,* Justin explained his now-famous discovery. "All my friends in the car, like 18-year-old guys, [are] singing this song and I'm like, 'Who *is* this person?'"

When Justin got back home, he looked up the singer, Carly Rae Jepsen, online. He was impressed with the then-26-year-old Carly's professional accomplishments. In 2007 she had placed third on *Canadian Idol* before the release of her first album, *Tug Of War,* the following year. In 2011, she debuted the video of "Call Me Maybe." This was the song that caught Justin's attention! Justin called his manager, Scooter Braun, and encouraged him to listen to "Call Me Maybe." Meanwhile, Justin tweeted about Carly to friends and fans.

Carly and Justin on stage together at 102.7 KISS FM's Wango Tango

"**Call me maybe by Carly Rae Jepsen is possibly the catchiest song I've ever heard lol.**"
— JUSTIN BIEBER'S TWEET WHEN HE FIRST HEARD "CALL ME MAYBE"

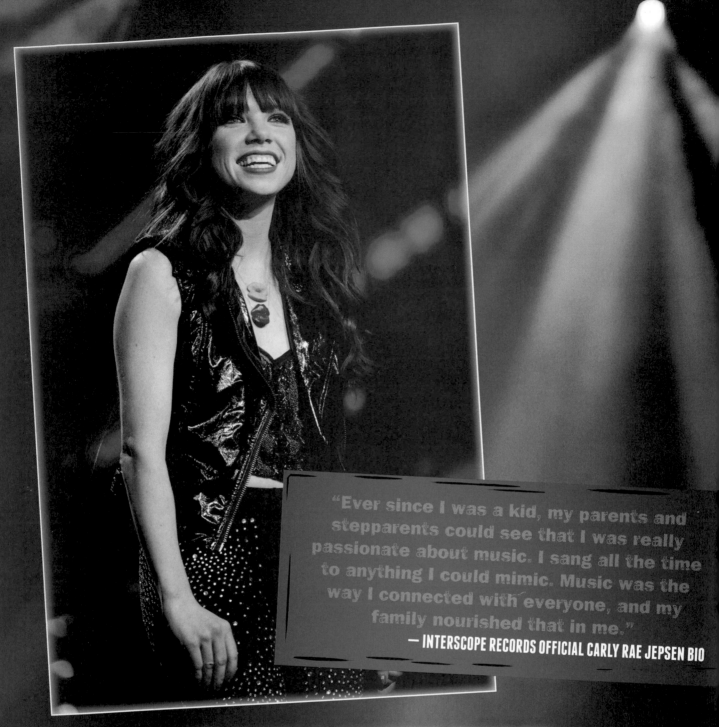

> "Ever since I was a kid, my parents and stepparents could see that I was really passionate about music. I sang all the time to anything I could mimic. Music was the way I connected with everyone, and my family nourished that in me."
>
> — INTERSCOPE RECORDS OFFICIAL CARLY RAE JEPSEN BIO

HER WORLD CHANGED FOREVER

Carly found out about Justin's interest from her sister, Kate, who was on Twitter when Justin tweeted Carly's song.

After that tweet, Carly's world changed forever. Scooter got in touch with her, they discussed her career, and he signed her to School Boy Records, the new label he had just launched with Justin. Days later, the singer flew to California to meet Justin. "I had no idea what to expect, and he blew away all my expectations," she told *Access Hollywood.*

Discovered by Justin Bieber...signed to his label...appearing with him at publicity events... and opening for him at concerts—"It's very surreal to me at times, because I think back to maybe two years ago and my career then versus now," Carly told the British newspaper *The Sun.* "The first time that I toured Canada was in [a] soccer-mom van, with the boys that I'm still playing stadiums with now. I was paying them with home cooked dinners because that's all I could afford, and rushing to my merchandising table to sell shirts afterwards."

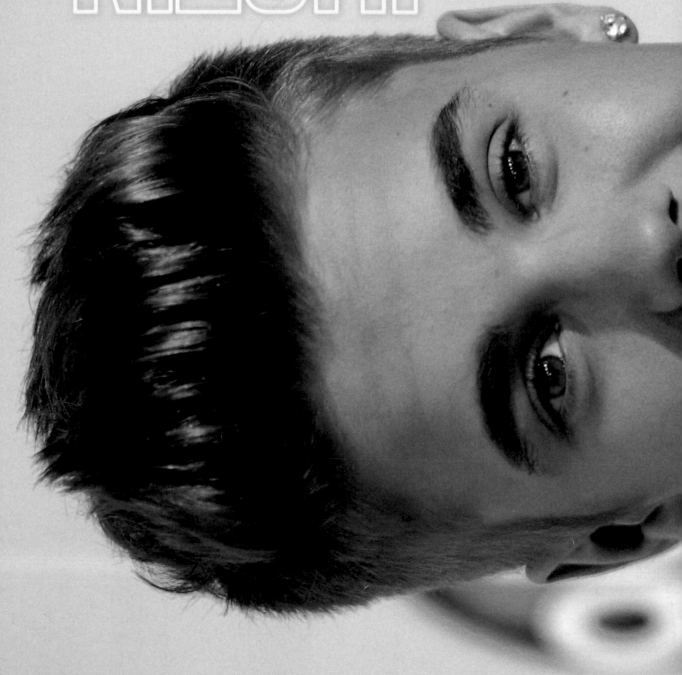

BIEBER

JUSTIN

Playing to a sell-out crowd at the legendary Madison Square Garden in New York City is a gigantic achievement for any artist. In *Justin Bieber: Just Getting Started*, Justin recalls, "For me, it became important because of Taylor Swift. Now, you might be wondering why it was Taylor who got my attention…The answer is pretty simple. The Garden is where I first saw her perform to a sell-out crowd in August 2009. Plus, that was my first time seeing a real arena show with an audience full of fans with their hands in the air connected to the artist. That night I looked at Scooter while we were standing in the pit and said, 'This is what I want to do for the rest of my life.'"

FROM THE BEGINNING, DOING WHAT SHE LOVED

Though Carly was doing what she loved and gathering fans across Canada, her career was not on a superfast track before Justin appeared on the scene. She had to supplement her income by taking side jobs as a pastry chef assistant, a waitress, and a nanny. Then, with the help of her mentor, her career exploded. "I remember feeling the growing pains in Canada, but I really wanted it to be like this," she told *Billboard,* talking about how things had changed so quickly for her. "I feel like I've gotten to go through the awkward years in my hometown and in my country, in Canada, and to take the time to develop the artist that I am, the music that I want to be putting out there. In a way, I felt like the timing couldn't have been better—right when I'd come to this peak of honing it in and having all of the experiments that succeeded and failed. It was nice to feel confident in what I was doing and feel like I really liked it. And to have someone like Justin, and of course Scooter, come along and say, 'What you're doing, we don't want you to change it, we just want to share it in a bigger way,' it was just really cool."

ALL CARLY, ALL THE TIME

During the summer of 2012, it was hard to go anywhere without hearing "Call Me Maybe" on the radio, on TV, on YouTube (the original and multitudes of covers), blasting through stores in malls…everywhere! *Billboard* named "Call Me Maybe" the "Song of the Summer," beating out Maroon 5's "Payphone," Gotye's "Somebody That I Used to Know," Katy Perry's "Wide Awake," and Ellie Goulding's "Lights."

"Call Me Maybe" allowed Carly to fulfill a longtime wish. "It's been a dream of mine to travel Europe as an adult since I went there when I was 11, but never imagined I'd be there for music," she told the *New York Post* about her overseas publicity tour. "I spent seven days in London, did a couple of photo shoots there, then went to Germany, France, and Australia. I think the travel has been the best part of all this, to be honest."

NO MAYBE ABOUT IT!

Among the high points of Carly's success in the year since Justin heard her on the radio have been nine weeks at number one on the Billboard Hot 100 chart for "Call Me Maybe," her MTV Video Music Award nomination for the single, and the September 2012 release of her second album, *Kiss,* which debuted at number six on the *Billboard 200* chart. And that month she hit the road opening for none other than Justin Bieber on his *Believe Tour.*

It may look as if Carly is an overnight success, but the truth is that she has put in years of hard work to get where she is today. Now is her time to shine, and no one agrees more than Scooter Braun. Recalling when they first started working together, he told *Billboard,* "I sat down Carly in my backyard and said, 'This is not going to be fun. You're going to be so tired. And she looked at me and said, 'Scooter, I don't care how hard I have to work. I'm going to do it. This what I've wanted my entire life.'"

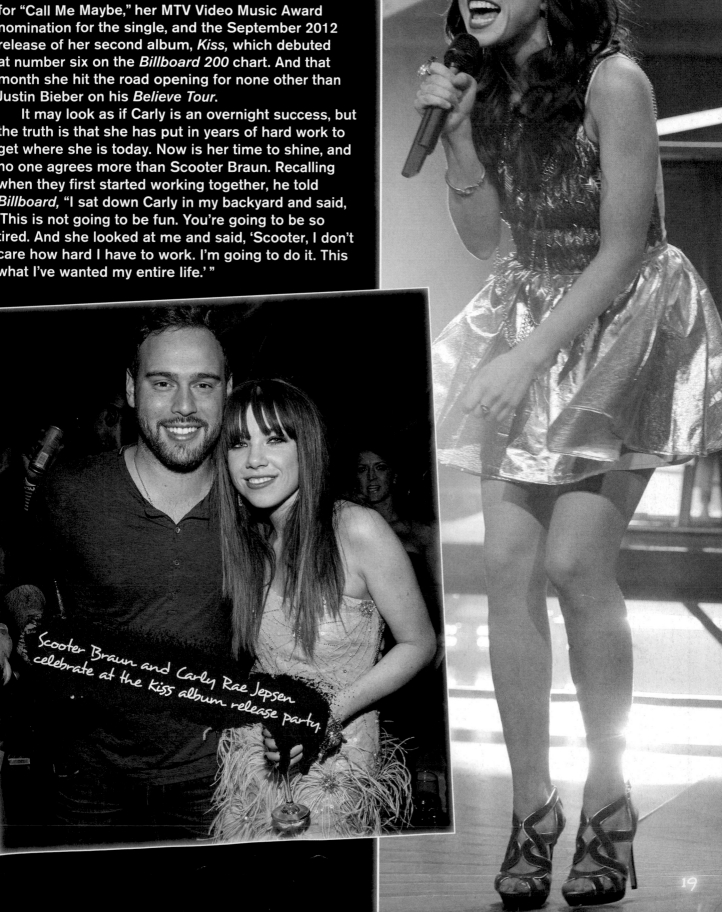

Scooter Braun and Carly Rae Jepsen celebrate at the Kiss album release party.

19

JADEN SMITH

— GREAT EXPECTATIONS —

As the son of superstars Will Smith and Jada Pinkett Smith, Jaden Smith, 14, grew up as Hollywood royalty. If he wants to follow in his parent's footsteps and perform, piece of cake, right? Well, yes and no. While some doors may fly open for him, landing roles is not enough. Will and Jada expect a lot more from Jaden as well as his younger sister Willow.

The parents of these two talented teens are setting the bar high. "I want [them] to live in service to greatness," Will told Oprah Winfrey in an OWN interview, discussing what he and Jada hope for their kids. "I want them to live and to create in a way that when people see it, people are inspired and people become better just by having contact with their excellence."

Jaden back in 2006

A COUNTRY GIRL

f anyone had told Taylor Swift 10 years ago that she would have a shelf full of music awards, she might have laughed it off as crazy talk. The odds would seem stacked against a little girl growing up on a Christmas tree farm in rural Pennsylvania. When her family moved to Wyomissing, a pretty suburb of Reading, PA, music played a major role in Taylor's life. She performed in musicals at the Berks Youth Theatre Academy and local fairs and festivals. She sang at sporting events, garden club galas, and coffeehouses, and competed in local talent contests. Clearly Taylor was gifted, but the fact that she preferred country music to pop set her apart from her suburban schoolmates.

"Junior high was actually sort of hard because I got dumped by this group of popular girls," Taylor told *Teen Vogue*. "The kids at school thought it was weird that I liked country [music]," she said. "They'd make fun of me."

In an interview with *Vogue*, Taylor recalled those days, "So…middle school? Awkward. Having a hobby that's different from everyone else's? Awkward. Singing the national anthem on weekends instead of going to sleepovers? More awkward. Braces? Awkward. Gain a lot of weight before you hit the growth spurt? Awkward. Frizzy hair, don't embrace curls yet? Awkward. Try to straighten it? Awkward….So many phases!"

Taylor back in 2006

DETERMINED TO SUCCEED

Though feeling different had been awkward, a trip to Nashville when Taylor was 11 resulted in rejections—and made her *want* to be different. She told *American Songwriter,* "Everyone in that town wanted to do what I wanted to do. So I kept thinking to myself, I need to figure out a way to be different."

Back home in Pennsylvania, Taylor learned how to play the guitar and focused on her songwriting, putting all those experiences of being an outsider and feeling different to good use. Pretty soon, a new, "different" Taylor landed a music manager. After appearing in an RCA Records showcase, she was signed to a development deal and was on her way. When she was 14, her father took a job transfer to Hendersonville, Tennessee— only a hop, skip, and jump from Nashville. At 15, Taylor signed with the independent label Big Machine and got a publishing deal for her songs with Sony/ATV Music, making her the youngest songwriter ever hired there.

In 2006, she released her first album, *Taylor Swift,* and became a country music star. There was nothing swift or easy about reaching that goal. "It didn't happen like it does in the movies," she told *American Songwriter.* "I look back and it seems like hundreds of thousands of tiny baby steps that led to that moment."

CONFESSION SESSION

In school Taylor knew she was different from her classmates. "I hated having curly hair because all the popular girls had straight hair. They'd make fun of me because my hair didn't look like theirs." Then, in ninth grade, she met another curly haired girl—Abigail Anderson—who soon became her BFF. "We never fit in with the cool girls at school—we were always a little odd, but we didn't care what people thought. We'd talk to each other in *Napoleon Dynamite* voices and go to dinner in our prom dresses, accessorized with scarves, fingerless gloves, tiaras, and funny slippers." — *Bop*

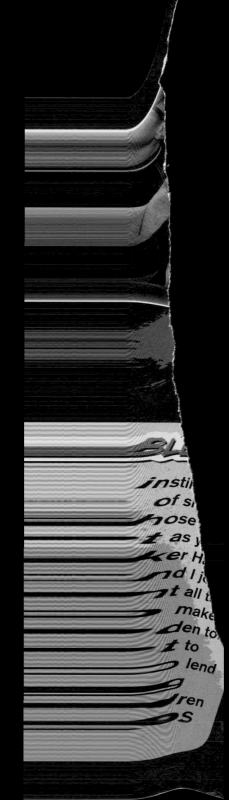

insti
of s
nose
t as y
er H
nd I j
t all t
make
den to
t to
lend

ren
s

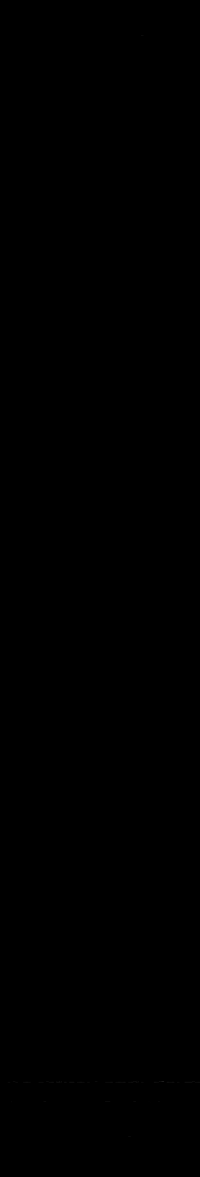

FROM THE HEART

What is the secret to Taylor's success? It may be that she writes songs about emotions and experiences she's dealt with herself. Feeling alienated from other girls, loving someone who treats her badly, falling for a boy who doesn't know she exists—these are the same issues girls go through every day. Taylor writes her own lyrics, sings songs from her heart, and her fans love her for it.

Taylor feels that along with her success comes a certain responsibility to behave as a role model—a responsibility she wholeheartedly embraces. "As you enter down a career path it becomes very clear what that career path is going to ask of you," Taylor told *Billboard* when it named her "Woman of the Year" in 2011. "One of the things that is a huge part of making music and putting it out into the world is understanding that you now have a role in shaping the lives of the next generation. And you can either accept that role or you can deny it and ignore it and say it's a parent's job to raise their kids. But the reality is what you wear matters. If you're a singer and on TV and in the living room of some 12-year-old girl she's watching what you're wearing and saying and doing. For me, when Faith Hill performed on an awards show, everything mattered—everything she said, did, wore, I tried to copy it. That's what little girls do, so there is a big responsibility and I take it very seriously."

RED ALERT! IT'S ALWAYS PERSONAL ⎯⎯

Describing the songs on her latest album, *Red,* Taylor told MTV News, "I tend to skew in the direction of writing songs and love-related things, relationship- and feeling-related things. That's where I naturally go.... There are things that I went through personally, and then there are stories I witnessed going on around me. When I'm writing an album, my world becomes a big storyboard and [everyone] has the potential to become a character and all my family and friends around me know that. The last two years have been really inspirational, and that's why there are so many songs on the album."

AUSTIN MAHONE

JUST SOMETHING TO DO

It was the summer of 2010 in San Antonio, TX. Fourteen-year-old Austin Mahone and his best friend, Alex Constancio, were hanging out in Austin's room, trying to figure out how to spend their summer vacation. Swimming? Biking? Shooting hoops? Nahhhh....Instead they spent the summer shooting videos of themselves and uploading them to YouTube—Austin and Alex doing silly comedy bits, showing off their "Dougie" dance moves, or whatever else they felt like doing that day. September rolled around, and it was back to school, but they didn't forget their summer project. In fact, they kept posting new videos to entertain their growing group of fans!

By early 2011, the boys expanded their content to music videos. As Austin told scholastic.com, "My first instrument was drums and I started playing that when I was 6, and then I played guitar at 14 and piano....The more I [played] music and practiced all those instruments, the more it just felt like this is what I wanted to do, and what was supposed to happen for me. ... I made a separate [YouTube] channel and just made covers of popular songs."

SOCIAL MEDIA SMARTS

In no time, Austin blew up. Hits on his videos grew every day. Soon local newspapers and TV stations began reporting on Austin. During his first TV interview with News 4 WOAI in November 2011, Austin said, "I started making videos with my best friend, Alex, in June of last year…me and Alex would get like 10 views a day, and we were so excited. Now in, like, two days I have like 80,000!"

And then those 80,000 views multiplied like crazy. As a matter of fact, Austin's cover of Justin Bieber's "Mistletoe" received more than 10,000,000 views, and it's still climbing! The next step was to post original material. On February 14, 2012, Austin put up his debut single, "11:11," a great Valentine's Day present for all his Mahomies.

Austin used YouTube as a grass roots base. Then he expanded his reach through Twitter, Facebook, and most important, Skype. As the number of Mahomies grew and demanded more availability to Austin, he and Alex set up Skype appointments. "I thought it would be cool to Skype with fans on their birthdays," Austin told *The Hollywood Reporter.* "I did a couple of two-hour Skypes.…I've had a lot of people tell me I'm doing something no one has ever done before."

29

AUSTIN BUSTS A MOVE

The June 2012 release of Austin's second single, "Say Somethin'," on YouTube and VEVO made him so popular he had to cut back on those regular Skype visits from his San Antonio bedroom because of demands on his time. *Billboard's Social 50* chart reported that "Say Somethin' " received over 1.5 million YouTube views the week of its release. His Facebook and Twitter followers increased by the thousands and his VEVO subscribers followed suit. Austin debuted at number 19 on *Billboard's Social 50* chart, which ranks artists by their popularity on YouTube, VEVO, Facebook, Twitter, and Myspace. Austin Mahone had definitely hit the big time.

With Austin's social media presence increasing exponentially, he was starting to get noticed. Some fans were calling him 'Baby Bieber" and 'The Second Coming of Bieber.' He may have started off goofing around during summer break, but now it was getting serious: in August 2012 the indie label Chase Records signed him.

Kara DioGuardi, who's had plenty of experience working with new talent as a former judge on *American Idol*, is a big Mahomie! She told *Hollywood Reporter*, "[Austin] knows how to connect. I think people feel attached to him because he's so genuine. He lets them into his bedroom and talks to them in his videos. He's got their notes on the wall….When you see him perform, it's like he's singing to you."

VIDEOS FOR FUN PAY OFF: "[Making music videos] just became one of my hobbies. It was what I would do in my spare time. I saw other people on YouTube making covers and I thought it was really cool and I just wanted to try it."

— TWIST.COM

BIEBER APPRECIATION ——

Austin does not deny using Justin Bieber and his success as a road map for his career. As a matter of fact, Austin will tell you that Bieber is someone he really looks up to, and when it comes to being compared with him, well, that's just fine. "It's flattering," Austin explained to mtv.com. "It's cool because he's such an inspiration to me and he's so successful, and I just hope that I'll be as successful as him someday."

Austin will never forget the time he actually met Justin Bieber! He was making his first visit to New York City's Z-100's *Elvis Duran and the Morning Show,* and he came face-to-face with the Biebs, who had just finished an interview with the DJ. "I got in an elevator, and he was standing right there," Austin told celebuzz.com. "He was a really cool dude."

But what was even better was that Justin gave Austin some words of wisdom before his radio interview with Elvis. "The advice that he gave me was that it doesn't matter how successful I get, I just gotta keep going and not be like, 'I made it here so I'm gonna stop working hard.' I gotta keep working harder and harder."

If he's guided by his role model, Austin will do just that—and then he'll never let his Mahomies down!

SELENA GOMEZ

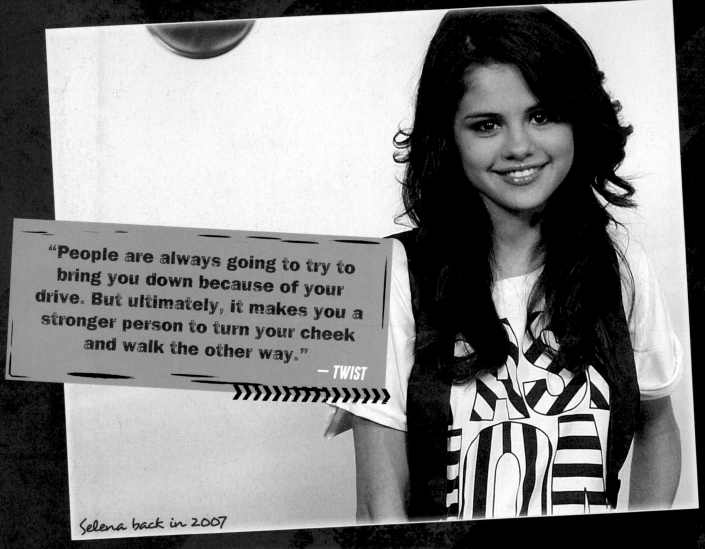

> "People are always going to try to bring you down because of your drive. But ultimately, it makes you a stronger person to turn your cheek and walk the other way."
> — *TWIST*

Selena back in 2007

HARD KNOCK BEGINNINGS

Growing up in Grand Prairie, TX, Selena Gomez faced early hardships. When she was 5, her parents divorced. Although both parents were in her life, Selena was raised by her mom, who worked long hours to support their household. Selena missed the early years when they would do things together as a family. "I wanted a family so bad," Selena revealed on *E! Entertainment Special: Selena Gomez.* "I wanted to have my dad and mom together. So it was really, it was really hard."

In addition to her split-family situation, something else set Selena apart from many of her peers. There wasn't much money, even though both parents worked hard. There were no weekly trips to the mall or dinners out. Selena's mom, Amanda, wanted to protect her daughter from the family's financial problems, and tried to provide Selena with some treats. "My mom saved up to take me to concerts," Selena told *Twist.*

But sometimes there was no way to hide from the reality. "I can remember…[times] when our car got stuck on the highway because we'd run out of gas," Selena said. It's hard to make believe everything is okay when you can't afford gas for the car!

A PURPLE DINOSAUR OPENS DOORS ———

Like any little girl, Selena had dreams. Hers centered around music and acting. Selena's mom felt she was talented, so she encouraged Selena's hopes of a show business career. When Selena was 7, she won the role of Gianna on the PBS TV series *Barney & Friends*, which is taped in Dallas. So Selena split her time between home, school, and *Barney*—but that caused a problem too. "I was bullied every second of every day in elementary and middle school," Selena told *Twist.* Selena realized the mean girls bullied her because they were jealous, but it didn't stop the hurt. Luckily she had a support system. "I had [two] best friends to go through that with, and it really helped me ignore the negative things I was hearing."

With support from her family and her BFFs, Selena turned the situation around. It made her stronger. And at 12, she was discovered at a nationwide Disney talent search. Selena was on her way to superstardom.

Selena and her mom, Amanda

FROM DINOSAURS TO *WIZARDS*

As a regular on *Barney & Friends,* Selena met another Texas belle, castmate Demi Lovato, who played Angela on the series. Their talent, and the desire to succeed that they shared, made them instant friends. After Selena and Demi had completed several seasons on *Barney & Friends,* their moms decided to take them to L.A. so they could pursue their careers there. "We didn't have that much money coming out here [to L.A.], so we were living together to share expenses," Selena told *Cosmopolitan.* "There were seven of us girls living in one loft, including sisters and moms and everything. It was really interesting."

Selena was the first to get a break, appearing as a guest star on the Disney Channel's top show at the time, *The Suite Life of Zack & Cody.* Next came a recurring role on Disney Channel's new hit, *Hannah Montana.* The Disney executives were so impressed with Selena they cast her in two pilots, *What's Stevie Thinking?*—a spin-off of Selena's favorite Hillary Duff show, *Lizzie McGuire*—and *Arwin!,* a spin-off of *The Suite Life of Zack & Cody.* Neither series was picked up, but Disney and Selena hit gold in 2007 when they cast Selena as Alex Russo, the lead character in *Wizards of Waverly Place.*

Selena and Minnie Mouse wave to their fans at the 2007 world premiere of High School Musical 2.

BEYOND *WIZARDS*

Selena's enormous popularity on *Wizards* opened musical doors beyond singing the show's theme song. In 2008, Disney signed her to Hollywood Records, their in-house label, and Selena sang on the soundtracks for other TV series such as *Shake It Up!*, and their films *Tinker Bell* and *Princess Protection Program*. In 2009, Selena formed her band, Selena Gomez & the Scene, which released three albums over two years: *Kiss & Tell, A Year Without Rain,* and *When the Sun Goes Down.*

Having achieved success in television and music, Selena has recently been concentrating on feature films. She's already appeared in movies including *Ramona and Beezus* and voiced characters in animated films like *Hotel Transylvania,* and she has several movies due for release in 2013. Discussing her career with *Teen Vogue,* Serena said, "Being part of the Disney Channel was such a blessing, and I'm super happy with what my show accomplished, but acting is something I would like to take on more seriously. I don't necessarily feel accomplished. I want to create a whole different persona when it comes to acting." Though Selena feels a responsibility as a role model to her fans, she doesn't want it to stop her from taking on more adult roles. "I am choosing roles and movies and music that might be a little different," she told *Cosmopolitan.* "But it's just me evolving and growing."

"You only live once, and I want to be proud of everything that I do and just have fun. I want to be able to say that I had a really fulfilled, fun life."
— COSMOPOLITAN

BIG TIME
RUSH

FOUR STRANGERS MEET

In 2009, the Nickelodeon network issued a casting call for singers and dancers. Logan Henderson, Carlos Pena Jr., Kendall Schmidt, and James Maslow were among the 1,500 people who showed up to audition. All four went through the grueling but ultimately rewarding process of returning for multiple callbacks. Finally, they each beat out the competition and were hired by Nickelodeon as members of the new band Big Time Rush—and as the stars of the new television series by the same name.

All four had prior acting and musical experience and each one had something unique and special to contribute to the group. But they needed to learn how to work as a team. Their opportunity came in an extended preproduction period for the series. The guys bonded and became exactly what the network intended them to be: four good friends who were totally at ease performing together.

Big Time Rush back in 2010

BTR AND 1D

Many fans want to know if the guys in BTR are tight with the 1D lads since they toured together earlier in 2012. James told justjared.com, "At the time both groups were really busy and it was actually hard to hang out with them. We made a point, I think it was in Chicago, that we basically said, 'You guys are staying after the show. We're locking ourselves in the dressing rooms and we're going to have a great time!' We basically had a little party and had fun. They did get us all soccer jerseys as a thank-you for opening for us on tour."

LOGAN

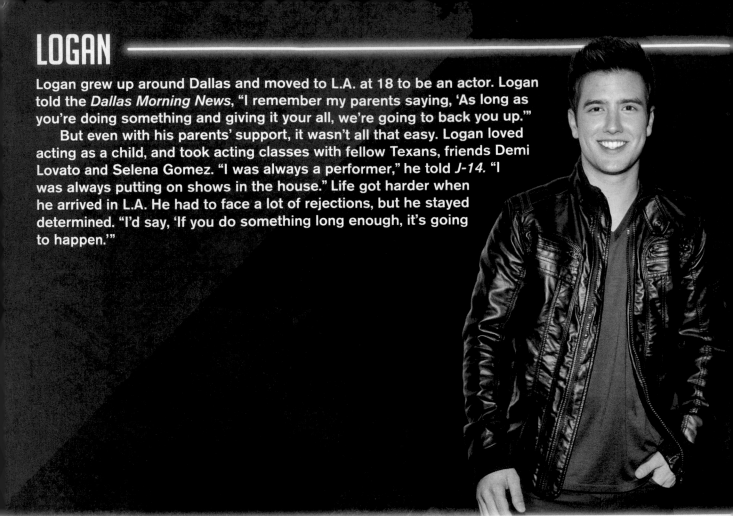

Logan grew up around Dallas and moved to L.A. at 18 to be an actor. Logan told the *Dallas Morning News*, "I remember my parents saying, 'As long as you're doing something and giving it your all, we're going to back you up.'"

But even with his parents' support, it wasn't all that easy. Logan loved acting as a child, and took acting classes with fellow Texans, friends Demi Lovato and Selena Gomez. "I was always a performer," he told *J-14*. "I was always putting on shows in the house." Life got harder when he arrived in L.A. He had to face a lot of rejections, but he stayed determined. "I'd say, 'If you do something long enough, it's going to happen.'"

CARLOS

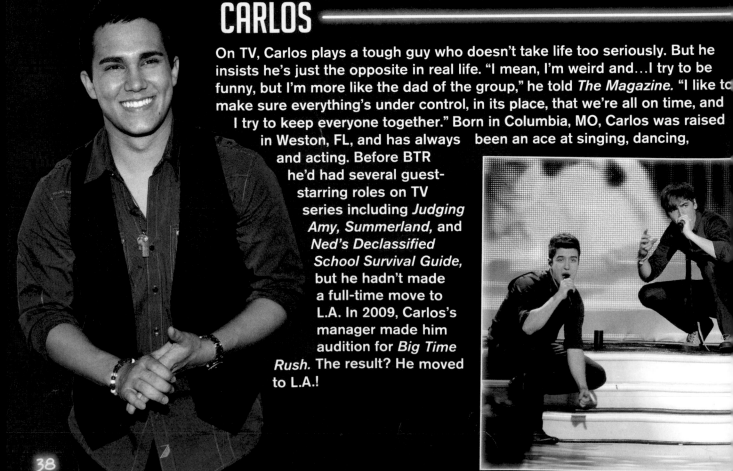

On TV, Carlos plays a tough guy who doesn't take life too seriously. But he insists he's just the opposite in real life. "I mean, I'm weird and…I try to be funny, but I'm more like the dad of the group," he told *The Magazine*. "I like to make sure everything's under control, in its place, that we're all on time, and I try to keep everyone together." Born in Columbia, MO, Carlos was raised in Weston, FL, and has always been an ace at singing, dancing, and acting. Before BTR he'd had several guest-starring roles on TV series including *Judging Amy, Summerland,* and *Ned's Declassified School Survival Guide,* but he hadn't made a full-time move to L.A. In 2009, Carlos's manager made him audition for *Big Time Rush.* The result? He moved to L.A.!

JAMES

James told bopandtigerbeat.com that he's not much like his appearance-obsessed TV character. "My character...[is] always trying to make new fashion statements." But the real James? "Whatever is clean, I wear." James was born in New York City and moved with his family to La Jolla, CA, when he was 6. He fell in love with acting early on. "When I was 13, I went to a performing arts school and I wasn't exercising much," he told *J-14*. "So I had baby fat for several years beyond the acceptable years of baby fat."

James remembers being teased and called "Fatso." It hurt his feelings, but it also made him do something about it. "I went to the gym and learned how to exercise properly," he said. "It wasn't fun to be made fun of." By the time James graduated in 2007, he looked very much like the cute guy we know today. He made his TV debut in 2008 on *iCarly*.

KENDALL

While his fellow BTR members consider Kendall the shy one of the group, he calls himself "the rocker." Born in Wichita, KS, he grew up in nearby Andover, where he held odd jobs like working in a pet store before going into acting. He's actually the thrid Scmidt brother who acts; he was bitten by the bug after his older brothers Kenneth and Kevin began traveling to Hollywood for gigs.

At age 9, Kendall was one of Haley Joel Osment's body doubles in *A.I. Artificial Intelligence,* and when he was 10, his whole family made the move to L.A. Kendall scored a slew of recurring roles, including ones on *General Hospital* and *Gilmore Girls,* before hitting it big with *Big Time Rush.* (BTW, *BTR* casting directors were impressed by Kendall's agile and acrobatic dancing on his audition tape.)

FOUR FRIENDS WORK TOGETHER

Four strangers became four fast friends through the music they made together. It makes sense that the boys of BTR and the boys of One Direction get on as well as they do. They have a lot in common!

Many BTR fans have been asking if there is any chance that BTR would tour with One Direction again or even do a duet with 1D. The BTR bunch said they would be up for it, though at the moment

1D is busy promoting their new *Take Me Home* album. Carlos spoke fondly of the 1D crew to *Bop*—"They're awesome guys. They have a similar sense of humor to us, and they're enjoying the rise. They love their fans."

As for BTR, "We're going to be a band as long as our record label allows us to," James told justjared.com in 2012. "We don't have any set

"For us, even to say hi to someone, to change their day around or change something inside of them— that's a pretty cool feeling." — LOGAN , PARADE.COM

...ates on when we're going to really try to work ...n our own stuff. We're dedicated to BTR until the ...ery end, and we don't even know when that is." ...he guys' devotion to each other was summed up ...n a quote by Logan to parade.com, "We argue like ...rothers, but we love each other."

The band is devoted to filming its show, doing ...oncerts, and making personal appearances,

where the guys often make the time to meet their fans one-on-one.

Fans can expect more music from the band and more TV, too. Their Nickelodeon series began its fourth season in early 2013 and BTR's third studio album has been scheduled to drop the same year.

LADY GAGA

Lady Gaga back in 2007

QUIRKY GIRL IN A NYC WHIRL

A former student of Manhattan's Convent of the Sacred Heart spoke to *New York Magazine* in 2010 and described her classmates' behavior toward Stephani Germanotta, aka Lady Gaga. "[They] talked behind her back, like, 'Gross, she's the Germ! She's dirty!'" Gaga felt bullied, but later on she drew on that experience to create a relationship with her fans. "I didn't fit in in high school, and I felt like a freak," Lady Gaga said on *The Ellen DeGeneres Show.* "So [now] I like to create this atmosphere for my fans where they feel like they have a freak in me to hang out with and they don't feel alone."

Gaga dressed to please herself, not other girls, and they made fun of her for it. She told *Vanity Fair,* "I was very much like my mother; she would do her hair every morning and get dressed nice.... So...I just liked to be glamorous. It made me feel like a star." Gaga told *Time,* "My courage and my bravery at a young age was the thing I was bullied for, a kind of 'Who do you think you are?'"

She knew that it was okay to be an outsider in the music world and being different could actually help her succeed. Her open-minded parents didn't stand in the way of their future superstar. She told *V,* "There was no stopping me. I was always in a moment of performance and creativity. My parents encouraged me in that they never tried to change me....But in a way, my home has always been the stage. I was the girl...too busy finishing a chord progression or lyric, dreaming of...becoming a superstar."

ONE YEAR OR BACK TO SCHOOL

After high school Gaga became one of 20 early admission students to New York University's prestigiou Collaborative Arts Project 21. Studying what she loved—music, art, theater, and literature—she seemed to thrive, but mid–sophomore year, she dropped out. "I left my entire family, got the cheapest apartmen I could find, and ate [junk] until somebody would listen," she told *New York Magazine*.

Her father agreed to pay her rent for one year. They had a deal—if she didn't make it in the music business by the end of that year, she would return to NYU. Still known as Stefani at the time, she collaborated with a number of cutting-edge artists on the downtown scene. She wrote her own music, played clubs, and sent demos to every record label she could think of. Her style at the time was electro pop. Finally, she caught the ear of an executive from Def Jam Recordings and was signed to a label with her new name, "Lady Gaga." When Def Jam dropped her contract after only three months, she *still* didn't give up. She reinvented herself, focusing her musical talents on pop-glam rock. When an executive at Interscope Records heard Gaga's new sound he loved it and signed her up. This time her label stuck.

FEELIN' FREE, GAGA-STYLE —

When does Gaga feel that she's the most herself? Apparently not when she's alone—as some people might think. "Onstage, especially at the piano," is what she told *V*. "The most defining moments of liberation always occur when I am performing a new song for the first time."

BEST FACE FORWARD

After three successful albums and a fourth album on the way for 2013, sold-out tours, a MAC cosmetic campaign, and lots and lots of charitable work, Gaga told *Vanity Fair* that she's still in love with being a pop star: "I love to sing. I love to dance. I love show business. I need it. It's like breath."

Lady G has started a new body-image campaign—via her official site—called A Body Revolution 2013. She created it after being criticized by the media about a sudden weight gain in the early fall of 2012. Gaga released photos of herself at her heaviest, beginning with one picturing her dressed in a yellow bra and underwear, with the caption, "Bulimia and anorexia since I was 15."

After revealing that she had battled eating disorders, she announced on her website that she wanted to reach out and support Little Monsters who might be dealing with them as well. "When I eat and am healthy and not so worried about my looks, I'm happy. Happier than I've ever been. I am not going to go

on a psycho-spree because of scrutiny. This is who I am. And I am proud at any size," she said, encouraging others to be proud of their unique shapes, too. "Be brave and celebrate with us your 'perceived flaws,' as society tells us. May we make our flaws famous, and thus redefine heinous."

Followers of Gaga's site were quick to post their own stories about body issues and eating disorders. Once again she had reached out and connected with her fans in her special way. This Lady's not only a musical legend, but also a great friend when it comes to making her fans feel understood!

"I think that fashion and music go hand-in-hand, and they always should. It's the artist's job to create imagery that matches the music...I think they're very intertwined."
— ARTISTDIRECT.COM

THINK ABOUT IT...

"Don't you think that what's on the cover of a magazine is quite artificial?" Lady Gaga asked *Harper's Bazaar*. "There's this idea that it's all natural, but everything's been staged to look natural. It is also an invention. It's just that my inventions are different. I often get asked about my artifice, but isn't fashion based on the idea that we can create a fantasy?"

NE-YO

Ne-Yo back in 2005

SURROUNDED BY WOMEN AND MUSIC

haffer Chimere Smith (aka Ne-Yo) spent his arly years in Camden, AK. When he was a little oy, his parents separated and his mom, Lorraine urts, moved her son and his little sister, Nikki mith, to Las Vegas. She felt the move would ive her family a fresh start. It also meant he was urrounded by women—his mom, his sister, his randmother, and five aunts! We're betting he got lot of attention.

From early on Ne-Yo showed a sensitive side. wasn't into basketball and football and fixing ars," he told *USA Today.* "I was into painting and rawing and poetry." Music filled the house day nd night, and it often touched him. Ne-Yo told *terview,* "I remember when I was a kid and my other used to play 'Suddenly' by Billy Ocean. I sed to cry like my dog had just died."

Though Ne-Yo's mom encouraged him to pursue his creative side, it wasn't all that easy. He loved singing, but he had a major problem with it. "I hated my voice," he told *USA Today.* "I thought it was too high and tinny and nasal. I wanted to have more of a growl, you know?" But his mom helped him accept his voice by asking him to listen to artists including Michael Jackson and Stevie Wonder. "She said, 'Study these artists, because their tone is similar to yours, and you'll find your own voice.' And sure enough, I did," said Ne-Yo.

Ne-Yo credits his mom for giving him, by advice and example, the tools he needed to pursue his dreams. "She is the strongest woman on the face of the planet," he told *USA Today.* "I've seen her go through unimaginable obstacles, and you would never know she had a bad day in her life."

49

ALWAYS WRITING

Ne-Yo wanted the chance to show what he could do, not only as a singer, but also as a writer. "I used to walk around with a journal when I was young, writing down just pretty much everything that happened to me throughout the day," he told thestarscoop.com. "Just the whole art of writing, it wasn't even songs in the beginning, it was journal entries, poems, short stories, and then eventually it became songs."

Later on, the qualities and talents that first set Ne-Yo apart from his sport- and car-obsessed schoolmates turned him into Mr. Popular. While still attending high school at Las Vegas Academy, Ne-Yo joined an R&B group called Envy. The group drew local attention and also sparked interest from record labels. When Envy broke up in 2000, Ne-Yo continued on his own. At only 20, Columbia Records signed him as a solo artist. But signing with a label wasn't the dream come true that he thought it would be.

A newcomer to show business, Ne-Yo was in the hands of his label creatively. As work progressed on the album, he didn't like the direction the label was taking him. "At 19 or 20, I decided I would let them create me, and in the process I figured out I wasn't the person they wanted me to be," he told *USA Today*.

Unfortunately, Ne-Yo's relationship with Columbia ended with a shelved album and a cancelled contract. But he wasn't about to let *that* spell the end of his career.

>>>>>>>>>>>>>>>>>>>>>>>>

"I make it my business to not really write songs about stuff that I don't know anything about. So, pretty much every song I've ever written has come from either personal experience or experiences from someone close to me, you know. I just think the song comes out better when you know a little bit about what you're writing about. That's where my inspiration comes from."

— THESTARSCOOP.COM

51

IN HIS OWN WORDS ———

After Ne-Yo was dropped from his first label, he decided to focus on his songwriting talents and penned songs for major artists such as Janet Jackson, Celine Dion, Marques Houston, Mary J. Blige, Faith Evans, and Enrique Iglesias. Ne-Yo got a major break when Mario recorded his song "Let Me Love You" and it went to number one on *Billboard.* Island Def Jam Recordings' L.A. Reid approached him to join its roster of recording artists. "L.A. said, 'I signed you because I like what you do,'" Ne-Yo told *USA Today.* "He wrote me a check and said, 'Here's your recording budget. Come back when you have an album.' He gave me complete control."

Ne-Yo's first album, *In My Own Words,* was released in early 2006, debuting at number one on the *Billboard 200* album chart. His second single from the album, "So Sick," went to number one on the *Billboard 100* singles chart. His other albums—*Because of You, Year of the Gentleman, Libra Scale,* and *R.E.D,* released in late 2012—have been just as successful.

"I want to write short stories, poems, scripts. I want to do a screenplay and a theater play. I want to do it all."

— *USA TODAY*

MULTITALENTED

A multiplatinum artist in his own right, Ne-Yo still writes for other artists—Jennifer Hudson, Mary J. Blige, Beyoncé, Justin Bieber, Cheryl Cole, Willow Smith, and Monica, to name just a few. And on *R.E.D.* he collaborated with Tim McGraw and Wix Khalifa, and for the album's deluxe edition, with Fabolous and Diddy.

In 2012, Ne-Yo moved to Motown Records and now, along with making musc, works for the label. His executive responsibilities include finding and mentoring new talent for the label and working as a producer with other Motown artists. On top of all this, Ne-Yo opened his own recording studio, Carrington House, in 2007 in Atlanta.

Ne-Yo knows all his success wouldn't be possible without his fans. He told thestarscoop.com: "The fans are the most important thing, period...because these are the people that make me who I am. If not for them, I would be making music in my basement for nobody to listen to but myself."

KATY PERRY

HELLO, KATY—POP PRINCESS IN TRAINING

Katy Perry's early beginning as a singer was not what you might expect for a pop star with such a distinctive—and often racy—fashion sense, who sings such catchy tunes. Her parents, traveling ministers, forbade her to listen to pop and rock music. From the time she was 9 until she was about 17, Katy (born Katheryn Elizabeth Hudson) showed off her voice singing in church. Recognizing her gift, Katy's parents paid for vocal lessons. As time went on, Katy was so sure she wanted a singing career, she dropped out of high school after her freshman year (eventually earning her GED) so she could spend more time focused on her goal.

At 15, Katy signed to a Christian label, Red Hill, under the name Katy Hudson (she later changed it so she wouldn't be confused with the actress Kate Hudson) and released a self-titled gospel-rock album in 2001. It didn't sell well. Undaunted, Katy left home at 17 for L.A. and spent the next few years working on both her songwriting and singing with producer Glen Ballard. Ballard told *Rolling Stone,* "When Katy's father brought her into my studio, I thought she was just going to hand me some music to hear. But then she came with her guitar and sat right down to play me a song. At that moment, I thought she was extraordinary. She's never had any fear."

Katy back in 2008

"My family is definitely very supportive. I have, I guess, pushed their envelope from the day I was born. I was always the kid at the dinner table who, if there was a line you shouldn't cross, I took a big leap over it. That's always been me. There's never really been, like, an edit button on my keyboard of life. I guess my parents weren't ever so shocked when I was singing very frank or honest, to me honest, songs."

— BELIEFNET.COM

Over the next five years, deals with Island Def Jam and Columbia ended in disappointment, too. But she kept at it. She sang background on a Mick Jagger solo record, and had a song on the sound track for *The Sisterhood of the Traveling Pants.* She was working, but still no solo album. Finally in 2007, Virgin Records chairman Jason Flom heard some of her original songs. He saw (and heard) in Katy Perry the makings of the next pop princess.

When "I Kissed a Girl," one of two singles she wrote with writer-producer Dr. Luke, was released in May 2008, the kitty was out of the bag—Katy had a number-one single and was on her way to superstardom! *One of the Boys* dropped in June 2008, to great reviews. She took off on a two-month promotional tour for *One of the Boys,* and members of the media seemed just as impressed with her charismatic personality and natural quirkiness as they were with her music.

"You have a huge hit song and everybody...knows who Katy Perry is. What people don't know is what you've gone through...to get to that point...[that] you were dropped by three record labels."

— *THE ELLEN DEGENERES SHOW*

TEENAGE DREAMS COMING TRUE ─────

When asked by mtvasia.com to describe her second album, *Teenage Dream,* released in August 2010, Katy said, "*Teenage Dream* is a perfect snapshot into who I am in general—as a young woman, with my perspectives, convictions, anthems, and mottoes....It's full of different dimensions. It has songs like 'California Gurls' that are really fun and obvious and then there are songs like 'Firework' that would hopefully motivate you and make you want to move and there are songs like 'Not Like the Movies,' which is a love song."

While Katy's been turning heads as a recording artist, she's also done so with her unique sense of style. No wonder—she's as fiercely individual about fashion as she is about her music. From her rainbow-bright hair colors to her cartoonish stage costumes, it's all a part of her larger personal appeal, which was all on display in her movie, *Katy Perry: Part of Me.* "I just like to have my own kind of direction when it comes to things I wear," says Katy. Katy has a lot for fans to love, not only her music but her incredible sense of self and dedication to her dreams.

INSPIRED KATY

"It's interesting...I meet a lot of different people who come from so many different places and they really kind of influence and inspire who I am....It does affect what I do musically and who I am as an entertainer...I think probably one of the things that is most important in life is not collecting all this stuff or trying to be as famous as possible but to worry about your soul and your spirit and what's happening next."
— mtvasia.com

58

"I'm a normal woman with big dreams who shows girls they can be a larger-than-life cartoon."
— *ROLLING STONE*

59

DRAKE

"When I think of myself, I think of Toronto. My music would never sound the way it does if it weren't for Toronto. You talk about certain artists, and they sound like where they're from."
— NOW TORONTO

Drake back in 2006

60

A COOL TWIST

Aubrey Drake Graham (aka Drake) was 5 when his parents divorced and his dad moved back to Tennessee. Drake was raised by his mom, a teacher, in Toronto. Though they were well-off financially, it was hard on Drake emotionally because he missed his dad. He also felt out of place because of his mixed race and religious background. As the son of a Jewish woman, Drake was Jewish, and as the son of an African-American father, he identified himself as black. "Nobody understood what it was like to be Jewish and black," he told *J-14.*

Sandi made Drake feel proud of his heritage even though he was teased by his schoolmates in their affluent neighborhood of Forest Hill. He and his mom celebrated the traditional Jewish holidays. By the time of his bar mitzvah at age 13, his peers were more accepting of his mixed heritage. Still, the rapper told *J-14,* "I never had a girlfriend. Not one of those girls would want to bring me home [to meet her family]. It would be too risky." Interestingly, Drake's narrow-minded schoolmates may have contributed to his career as a rapper. Their negative attitudes helped him develop a thick skin. Drake told *J-14,* "The same kids that made fun of me are super proud [of me] now. And they act as if nothing happened...being Jewish is kind of a cool twist. It makes me unique."

A MEGASTAR WHO STILL DOES BAR MITZVAHS!

Drake reconnected with his Jewish roots in the spring of 2011 when he performed at a bar mitzvah in New York. He told *The Jewish Chronicle,* "I actually went and did a bar mitzvah for a family in New York. It was very nice, and they were an incredible family to deal with...I loved it, man—the kids loved it, the parents loved it."

Drake and his mom, Sandi

CHARMING HIS WAY TO HIP-HOP HEIGHTS

Rapping was not Drake's first job in the entertainment world. Beginning at age 15, Drake spent seven seasons on the TV series *DeGrassi High: The Next Generation,* playing the wheelchair-bound, former basketball star Jimmy Brooks. He told *GQ* that he got the role after finding an agent through a schoolmate. "This kid in my class was like, 'Yo, my dad is an agent,'" he recalled. "'You should go talk to him because you're good and you make people laugh.' When it comes to knowing what to say, to charm, I always had it."

But Drake preferred music to acting. He told *GQ,* "[Rapping]...that's all I wanted to do, at first. I loved music. I just didn't necessarily believe in music being the focus right away...at 15, 16, 17, 18...I was really getting into that hip-hop phase and really studying the things that I needed to study as far as learning about flows and learning about lyrics."

Drake's studying paid off. His debut album, *So Far Gone,* entered the *Billboard 200* at number six and was the fifth-bestselling rap album of 2009. *Thank Me Later* (2010) and *Take Care (2011),* both debuted at number one on the *Billboard 200* and went platinum.

Now when Drake looks back, he realizes that his mixed background, the one that separated him from others growing up, is actually an asset to him as a performer. Drake observed in a colorlines.com interview, "I get a lot of love everywhere in the world for just being diverse, instead of just being straight out [one thing]. I'm all mixed up and people embrace that."

"I'm obsessed with perfection. I want to work. I don't want to take this for granted. I don't want to sit out here and say, 'Okay. I own this. You know, it's cool. I could stop.' But why? I don't want to stop. I want to take advantage and make myself the best possible me that I can be."

—GQ

63

RACHEL CROW

LOVE IS EVERYTHING

America fell in love with then 13-year-old Rachel Crow on the first season of *The X Factor.* Her free and bouncy hairstyle, her sparkling smile, her infectious laugh, and her never-ending enthusiasm were second only to the pull of her enormous talent. When she crumpled on the stage and sobbed on the night she was eliminated, her fans were devastated.

That kind of public collapse might have sent many performers running from the spotlight forever. Not Rachel Crow. The young talent whom judge L.A. Reid described as a "funky, feisty singer with soul," wiped her tears, composed herself, and bounced right back.

And *The X Factor* trial was not the first time Rachel proved she had major staying power. Rachel had already proved her determination as an infant. "She was born a crack baby," her adoptive mother, Barbara Crow, explained to *People.* "She went through withdrawals and everything."

The first months of Rachel's life were rough, but when Barbara and her husband, Kelly Crow, fostered and then adopted baby Rachel, things

ook a 180-degree turn toward the positive. Barbara
nd Kelly lived in the small town of Mead, CO, and they
howered Rachel with all the love and support anyone
ould want. Life only got better when Rachel was 3, and
er parents adopted another little girl, Hannah. Their
ight-knit family thrived. Rachel and Hannah were girly-
irls who loved family nights, playing games, and doing
hings together. The family also encouraged Rachel when
: became obvious that she had an awesome singing voice.
She got her first shot at a talent show when she was 5.
That was the moment I knew I wanted to pursue singing
rofessionally," she told *The Hollywood Reporter*.

FUN FACT!

Rachel's family lived on a
farm in Colorado. "I have two
miniature donkeys named
Blossom and Gabby," she
told *The Hollywood Reporter*
in April 2012. "We also have
a llama named Roy, and I
have lots of chickens! My
family has had a lot of pets,
including four horses, a
camel named Dalton, and
even a reindeer!"

STANDING UP TO BULLIES

When Rachel started school, she learned a universal, hard truth: not everyone is as loving as your parents. Some of her classmates picked on her for being a biracial girl adopted by a white family. "Kids would come up to me and say, 'Why are you different?'" Rachel told *J-14*. "They were just terrible to me. They told me that I was stupid."

Though Rachel's parents tried to help her through this bullying, Rachel remembers it was pretty hard. "It was the looks and the being called 'weirdo' and 'freak' [that hurt]," Rachel told aol.com. "Me and my one friend would stick together and just brush it off, but of course there were times when I would come home crying to my mom and saying, 'They called me this!' And she would say, 'Oh, they're just jealous!' But I was different in every possible way in school. I grew up in a very small, very conservative farm town....I was loud and outgoing and had curly hair, and they were just kind of like, 'What is going on right now? What is this creature?' I was just being myself and my parents taught me to always be myself and never think you have to be different than who you are. That was what made me confident to try out for *X Factor*. Honestly, looking back at it, I feel sorry for all the mean girls and bullies."

"I'm still just Rachel. I'm a pretty normal kid—except I've got this hair!"
— *PEOPLE*

LIFE AFTER *THE X FACTOR*

The X Factor did more for Rachel than increase her confidence. Even though she wasn't the winner, the show sparked a whole new life for her and her family. The Crows moved to Sherman Oaks, California, where Rachel was thrilled to have a room of her own for the first time. Rachel also signed with Columbia Records and became part of Team Nickelodeon. She opened for Big Time Rush during its 2012 summer tour, got a recurring role on Lucas Cruikchank's show, *Fred,* and reportedly is being groomed for a Nick show of her own. "It's amazing to think that a small-town girl like me can find themselves on Nickelodeon," she told the *Los Angeles Times.*

Rachel also released her debut EP, *Rachel Crow.* Based on the title, it's no surprise she cowrote the first single, "Mean Girls."

What Rachel hopes now is that her life, her songs, her voice will teach people what you are really supposed to do—love each other, be kind, and be happy. That's the Rachel way!

Rachel and Big Time Rush at the 2012 Nickelodeon upfronts.

TAYLOR LAUTNER

Taylor back in 2005

TOUGH GUY

Taylor Lautner was disciplined and determined from the start. When he was only 8 years old, he became a black-belt champion in karate. Three years later, intent on being an actor, he moved with his family from Grand Rapids, MI to the Los Angeles area to pursue roles. "I heard, 'No, no, no, no,' so many times," he told the *Grand Rapids Press.* "From karate, I had the confidence and drive to push myself." His perseverance paid off with small parts on TV shows like *The*

Bernie Mac Show, and in 2005 he landed the leading role of Shark Boy in *The Adventures of Shark Boy and Lava Girl 3-D.* At Valencia High School, he added football, baseball, and even hip-hop dancing to his schedule of activities, but busy as he was, he remained committed to his goal of making a name for himself as an actor. By the time he was 16, he had achieved it: He was a full-fledged star, melting hearts as werewolf Jacob in The Twilight Saga.

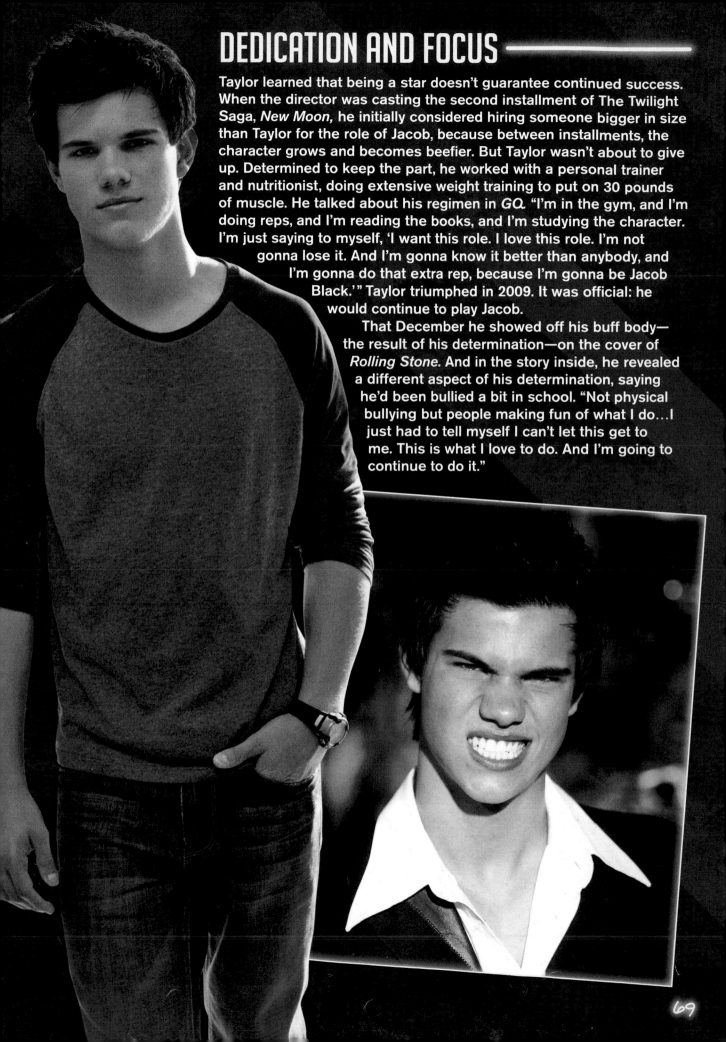

DEDICATION AND FOCUS

Taylor learned that being a star doesn't guarantee continued success. When the director was casting the second installment of The Twilight Saga, *New Moon,* he initially considered hiring someone bigger in size than Taylor for the role of Jacob, because between installments, the character grows and becomes beefier. But Taylor wasn't about to give up. Determined to keep the part, he worked with a personal trainer and nutritionist, doing extensive weight training to put on 30 pounds of muscle. He talked about his regimen in *GQ.* "I'm in the gym, and I'm doing reps, and I'm reading the books, and I'm studying the character. I'm just saying to myself, 'I want this role. I love this role. I'm not gonna lose it. And I'm gonna know it better than anybody, and I'm gonna do that extra rep, because I'm gonna be Jacob Black.'" Taylor triumphed in 2009. It was official: he would continue to play Jacob.

That December he showed off his buff body— the result of his determination—on the cover of *Rolling Stone.* And in the story inside, he revealed a different aspect of his determination, saying he'd been bullied a bit in school. "Not physical bullying but people making fun of what I do...I just had to tell myself I can't let this get to me. This is what I love to do. And I'm going to continue to do it."

HUMILITY AND GOALS —

The fifth and final film in The Twilight Saga was released in November 2012, and Taylor's life as Jacob came to a close. The actor is now recognized all over the world, but this is one performer who likes his privacy. And, though he's hard-driving and confident, he's not *over*confident. He's grateful for the opportunities he's had and he doesn't take them for granted. He's starred in one of the most successful film franchises in history—and earned acclaim as one of the sexiest werewolves ever—but he has no intention of resting on his laurels.

In 2013, Taylor will be seen in the comedy *Grown Ups 2,* and there will be more movies in his career that don't involve vampires and werewolves! He says he still has a long way to go. When *Seventeen* asked him where he wanted to be in five years, he said, "I believe in the saying, 'If you aim at nothing, you're going to hit nothing.' So if you don't set goals, then you have nowhere to go. I guess winning an Oscar is the ultimate dream. A lot of amazing actors go their whole career without even being nominated. So that would definitely be a goal to reach. It's a difficult one, but I'm aiming for it."

A DUDE WITH DRIVE!

"…You don't just go to bed and wake up the next morning and everything falls into place for you. It takes a lot of hard work to get to where you want to go." — *Seventeen*

"It comes down to what kind of mood you're in," Taylor told *GQ Australia*, referring to the fact that he's basically mobbed wherever he goes. "You have to make a decision before you go out: are you willing to sign autographs and take pictures, say hello and meet new people?...It gets frustrating. But during that frustration you say, 'OK. Why am I frustrated? I'm doing what I love.' But sometimes you really just want to go do whatever you want to do."

71

ROSS LYNCH

— HEARD HIM ON THE RADIO. . .AND SAW HIM ON TV! —

Growing up, Ross Lynch and his four talented siblings—Riker, Rocky, Ryland, and Rydel—loved to put on a show. They had taught themselves to play guitar, bass, drums, and piano, and they'd jam together just for fun, finally forming a homegrown band that played to local audiences. But the Lynch kids dreamed of making it in Hollywood. So in 2007 they moved out to L.A. with their parents, determined to pursue stardom.

Casting directors were immediately impressed by the Lynch bunch, who got dozens of commercials, theatrical projects, and music gigs. Then in 2011, Ross was cast in a Disney Channel sitcom pilot, *Austin & Ally*. He played the lead guy, Austin Moon, a teenage singer who posted a music video on the internet and turned into a superstar overnight—sound familiar? The pilot was picked up, and Ross was superstoked that he'd be writing a song for each episode. Two of them—"Heard It on the Radio" and "A Billion Hits"—created chart heat!

Austin & Ally became a big hit and was signed for a second season. Disney also tapped Ross for the lead role of Brady in the 2013 TV movie *Teen Beach Movie*.

For Ross, everything seems to be happening at jet speed, and he couldn't be happier. He welcomes all the tugs on his time and the chance to show off his talents—and he's determined to do it all.

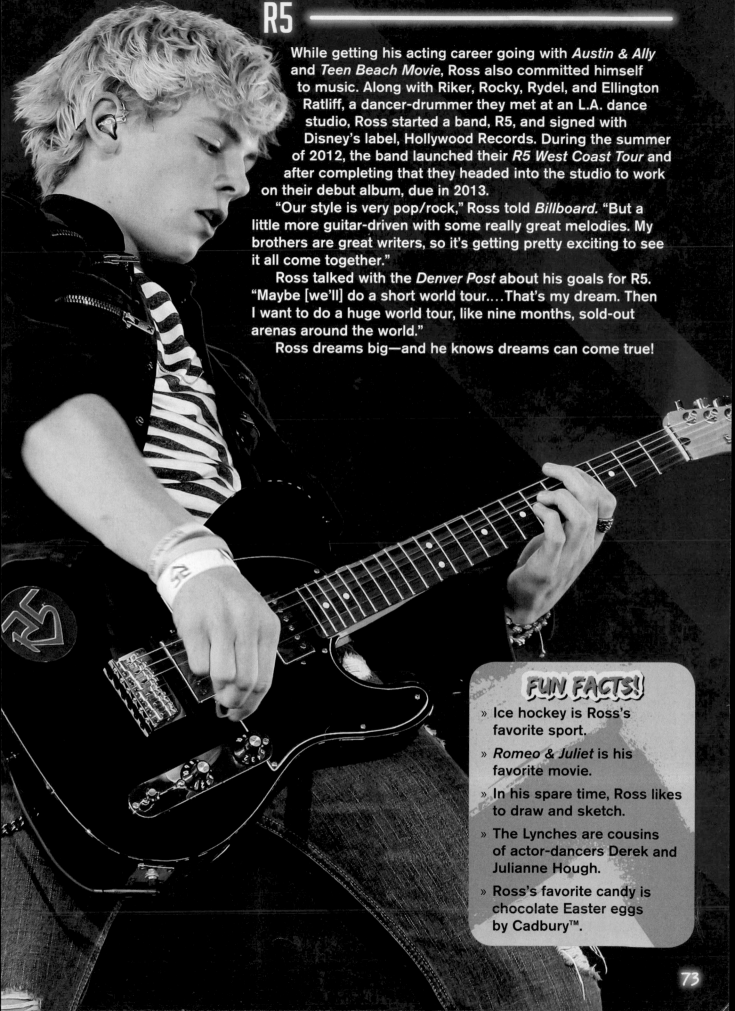

R5

While getting his acting career going with *Austin & Ally* and *Teen Beach Movie*, Ross also committed himself to music. Along with Riker, Rocky, Rydel, and Ellington Ratliff, a dancer-drummer they met at an L.A. dance studio, Ross started a band, R5, and signed with Disney's label, Hollywood Records. During the summer of 2012, the band launched their *R5 West Coast Tour* and after completing that they headed into the studio to work on their debut album, due in 2013.

"Our style is very pop/rock," Ross told *Billboard.* "But a little more guitar-driven with some really great melodies. My brothers are great writers, so it's getting pretty exciting to see it all come together."

Ross talked with the *Denver Post* about his goals for R5. "Maybe [we'll] do a short world tour….That's my dream. Then I want to do a huge world tour, like nine months, sold-out arenas around the world."

Ross dreams big—and he knows dreams can come true!

FUN FACTS!

» Ice hockey is Ross's favorite sport.

» *Romeo & Juliet* is his favorite movie.

» In his spare time, Ross likes to draw and sketch.

» The Lynches are cousins of actor-dancers Derek and Julianne Hough.

» Ross's favorite candy is chocolate Easter eggs by Cadbury™.

NICKI MINAJ

Nicki back in 2010

CINDERELLA DREAMS

When you see superstar rapper Nicki Minaj dressed up in all her wild and crazy glory, it's hard to imagine her as a poor 5-year-old kid with a troubled family life. Her parents broke up and got back together several times. She grew up hearing a lot of arguments between them. Nicki told *Allure,* "We would move all the time and whenever we pulled up to a house, I was hoping that this was the one—the one with the white picket fence. They were nothing like that."

Finally her mom took Nicki from their home in Trinidad-Tobago and moved to a tough neighborhood in Queens, New York. In some ways she traded one set of problems for another. She no longer had to watch her parents fight, but there was plenty of violence out on the streets of her neighborhood. Nicki had to find some kind of safe harbor. What made the future superstar strong was her belief in her musical talents. She attended LaGuardia High School, a theater-arts school, where she majored in acting. While going to school, Nicki rapped in a group called Hoodstars but left the group when it failed to get a record deal.

Even back then Nicki knew she had something special and was determined to make it—not so much for the fame and fortune, but to help her mom have a good life. "I would pray to God to make me famous so I could buy my mother a huge house," Nicki told *Cosmopolitan.* "I'd tell her, 'Let's go to a ballroom, like Cinderella.' She would laugh at me, but I knew I wasn't put here to be a regular person."

NEVER GIVE UP

Nicki was determined to make tracks in her career, so she got down to business and sent tapes to music-business execs. She is the first to point out that she was not an overnight success. She worked in various jobs—as a salesgirl, a cashier, and a waitress at Red Lobster—to pay the bills. But she didn't give up her musical ambitions. She believed in herself. Finally she was signed to a small independent label, Dirty Money Entertainment. Her mixtapes were so popular they prompted Universal Motown to offer her a deal, which she signed in 2009. Since then, her albums *Pink Friday* and *Pink Friday: Roman Reloaded* have debuted in the number one and two *Billboard 200*

spots respectively. Her success is a reminder to her fans—known as Barbz or Barbies—that they can be whatever they want to be. They just have to keep trying.

While becoming a hip-hop superstar, Nicki also became known for her distinctive approach to fashion. Nicki, who has been featured on the covers of magazines ranging from *Cosmopolitan* to *Billboard,* uses outlandish costumes, wigs, and makeup to make her style unforgettable. But underneath all that flash lurks a do-gooder who keeps quiet about a lot of her charitable activities. She regularly drops in at hospitals and schools to visit with kids. As a strong young woman who calls the shots, Nicki hopes to inspire her fans. This rapping Barbie is evidence that no matter where you come from, you can accomplish a lot with hard work and focus. There's no doubt that Nicki Minaj did it her way, and she believes others can too.

"[In 10 years] I'll have hundreds of millions of dollars. I will have put out five albums and I will have an Oscar and Grammys. And I will be getting married and, a couple of years after that, will have a bun in the oven"

— COSMOPOLITAN

77

LUCAS CRUIKSHANK

Lucas back in 201...

BOY WONDER

When Lucas Cruickshank was only 13, he created a character that would grow into a multimillion dollar industry: Fred Figglehorn, an angry 6-year-old who speaks in the high-pitched tones of Alvin the Chipmunk but deals with tough, real-life situations—a recovering-addict mother, a father he's never met who's on death row, a kid who bullies him. Working from his home in Columbus, Nebraska, Lucas and his cousins John and Katie uploaded the first Fred video for Halloween in 2006. Two years later Lucas got his own channel on YouTube and within a year a record-breaking one million subscribers had signed up!!

After Fred—and Lucas—became a phenomenon on the Web, they took their act to th big screen. *Fred: The Movie* aired on Nickelodeon in September 2010. Sequels followed, as well as *Fred: The Show*, a Nick TV series. Lucas serves as executive producer, and like many creative masterminds, he's very hands-on. "I oversee everything that goes on and just keep giving out notes," he told fanlala.com. "We've hired really good writers that know how Fred looks, how he sounds." Once there's a script, though, Lucas and

company often wing it. "I've always been interested in improv, and that's how Fred started out. Instead of going off of exactly what the script says, we just y improvising stuff and see what happens."

Lucas makes it all sound easy. He told the *New York Times* that it took only 30 minutes for im and his siblings—he has seven of them!—to reate each of the two-minute videos that started it l. "I just took how kids act in that age group and xaggerated it 100%," he said.

"[Fred fans] are surprised that my voice is normal and they're also surprised that I'm normal because they expect me to be just like Fred. They expect me to be all hyper and crazy."

— SEVENTEEN.COM

FRED'S EMPIRE

The story of Lucas's rise to fame is pretty amazing. He achieved something many adults have tried and failed to do. He leveraged his Internet popularity into TV and film success—transforming himself from a kid on YouTube into a bona fide entertainment mogul! And he did it all before he was out of his teens!

What's more, Lucas continues to expand his reach. In late 2012, *Marvin, Marvin* premiered on Nick, starring Lucas, as a new kid at school who's alientated from his schoolmates, mostly because—well, he's an alien! Lucas is also continuing his Fred TV movie franchise with Nickelodeon TV movies; the most recent was *Fred 3: Camp Fred.* He even has an endorsement deal with the makers of Zipit, an instant messaging device. When asked what roles he sees for himself in the future, Lucas says he wants to write, direct, and act in comedy films for adults.

He hopes his career will encourage other young, creative kids to do what he did—put videos up online for fun and see what happens. It also helps to put a lot of confidence, drive, and hard work behind those efforts, too! Just like Lucas.

Lucas and his friends, Matt Bennett, Daniella Monet, Gracie Dzienny, Rachel Crow, and Jeff Sutphen at the 2012 Nickelodeon World Wide Day of Play Celebration.

ONE DIRECTION

THIRD PLACE FEELS LIKE FIRST

Harry Styles, Liam Payne, Louis Tomlinson, Niall Horan, and Zayn Malik all auditioned in 2010 as solo acts for *The X Factor*. None of them advanced to the solo boys' round individually, so the judges suggested the five of them compete as a boy band in the group category, which Simon Cowell was mentoring that season.

"The minute they stood there for the first time together—it was a weird feeling," he told *Rolling Stone*. "When they came to my house in Spain and performed, after about a millionth of a second [I knew they would be huge]." When the

guys—now known as One Direction—returned to *The X Factor's* live shows, they didn't win. They came in third place. But no matter. Simon signed them to a deal on his Syco record label, and they headed right into the studio. Their first single, "What Makes You Beautiful," debuted at number one on the U.K. charts.

In late 2011 and early 2012, 1D found itself at the center of a whirlwind. After "What Makes You Beautiful" became the fastest-selling single of 2011 in the U.K., 1D followed it up with the U.K. release of its first album, *Up All Night*.

"We are so happy to be playing Madison Square Garden. To be headlining our *own* show in a venue that has played host to countless legendary acts that we have grown up listening to and adore is obviously a dream come true for us all."

— NIALL, *OK!*

hen they signed with Columbia Records in the J.S., released their album worldwide, and broke ales records almost weekly, immediately hitting umber one on *Billboard* in the U.S.

That feat itself made history—no other British roup had seen its first album debut at number ne in the U.S.. The rest of 2012 proved just as xciting. One Direction did mini-tours in Europe, ustralia, and the U.S.; sold over 12 million ecords worldwide in just the first half of the ear; won three MTV Video Awards and three een Choice Awards in the U.S. and other awards orldwide; and published two books, *Forever*

Young: Our Official X Factor Story and *Dare to Dream*. And then, they went back into the studio and recorded their second album, *Take Me Home*, which dropped in November 2012. What better way to celebrate an awesome year than by selling out their December show at Madison Square Garden in less than 10 minutes!

What does 2013 hold for the boys? Looks like they will spend the better part of the year working on their 3D movie, which Simon Cowell told mtv. com will not only "be about the fans" but will follow the boys on their huge 2013 world tour, which lands in the United States in June 2013.

WHEN THEY WERE SOLO

We know the boys clicked when they came together as One Direction. But what were they like before that time? What experiences made them want to become performers in the first place?

ZAYN

As a child, "I was really hyperactive and full of energy," Zayn told *Life Story*. But when he was about 7 or 8, he says, he found an outlet for his energy in music, joining a choir and then performing in school musicals. When Zayn was 15, a friend encouraged him to audition for *The X Factor*—but in the end he backed out. "I got too scared to audition, so I didn't go," Zayn told *J-14*. But a few years later, he had no choice but to go through with it. "My mom literally dragged me there," Zayn told *Seventeen*. "I was a very…quiet, reserved person. I loved singing, but I never had any major experience doing it….Not knowing what could happen was very daunting for me." He may have been nervous, but obviously Zayn made up for it with talent.

WAKE UP WITH 1D

Harry, Niall, Zayn, Louis, and Liam recently joined the Get Schooled Wake-Up campaign to encourage American kids not to skip school. Celebs including other superstars like Ciara and Chris Pine record wake-up messages that kids can sign up to receive every weekday morning. Hear that, sleepyheads? One Direction says, "Get up already!"

HARRY

Harry made his stage debut at the Happy Days nursery school in Cheshire, England, in his school's adaptation of *Chitty Chitty Bang Bang.* He also performed the role of a mouse who lived in a church in a production of *Barney.* Harry took to the spotlight immediately. "I always knew I wanted to kind of entertain people," he told *Life Story.* "I enjoyed showing off at school and was bit of an attention seeker." At 16—surprise surprise!—he headed off to audition for *The X Factor.* "I was young. It was a completely new thing for me....When we got put into a group, it was really cool and exciting, because we were all going through the same thing at the same time, which was amazing." Also amazing: he not only bonded with the spotlight, he bonded with four new friends!

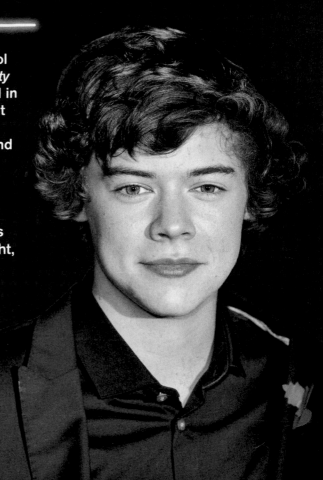

NIALL

Niall knew at a very young age—younger than his bandmates—that he wanted to sing professionally. "There are videos of me as a kid walking around singing and playing the guitar at maybe 4 or 5 years of age," he told *Life Story.* "I was always a singer and a mover."

Niall recalls a proud moment when he was singing in the car. His American aunt often visited Niall and his family in Ireland. "Once we were driving along, I was singing Garth Brooks in the back of the car," Niall told *J-14.* "She said she thought the radio was on!" That was encouragement enough for him!

Niall performed in school plays and musicals, and by the time he was in secondary school, began participating in local talent shows. But it wasn't until he had an opportunity to do *The X Factor* that Niall really thought he could turn his desire into reality, and make singing his career. And he sure hadn't thought about being in a group! But he jumped at the idea when it was presented to him. Good decision. As a member of 1D, he has fans everywhere—but his biggest fan is one of his first. "My auntie said she always knew I'd be famous," he told *J-14.* "She said it the entire time I was growing up, but I never thought anything of it." That's one smart auntie!

LIAM

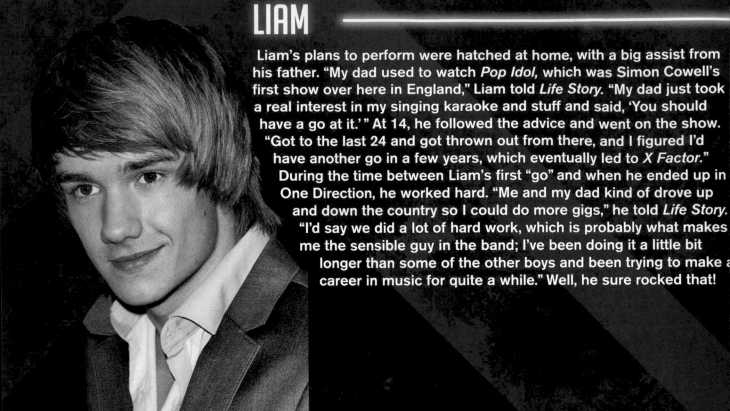

Liam's plans to perform were hatched at home, with a big assist from his father. "My dad used to watch *Pop Idol*, which was Simon Cowell's first show over here in England," Liam told *Life Story*. "My dad just took a real interest in my singing karaoke and stuff and said, 'You should have a go at it.'" At 14, he followed the advice and went on the show. "Got to the last 24 and got thrown out from there, and I figured I'd have another go in a few years, which eventually led to *X Factor*." During the time between Liam's first "go" and when he ended up in One Direction, he worked hard. "Me and my dad kind of drove up and down the country so I could do more gigs," he told *Life Story*. "I'd say we did a lot of hard work, which is probably what makes me the sensible guy in the band; I've been doing it a little bit longer than some of the other boys and been trying to make a career in music for quite a while." Well, he sure rocked that!

LOUIS

If it weren't for a teacher at Louis's high school, One Direction might have been a four-boy band! "A big influence on my career was a drama teacher," Louis told *J-14*. The school musical, a production of *Grease*—Louis had loved the film—was about to be cast. "I'd never been in a musical before, so I decided to audition for it." Louis won the lead role of Danny Zuko—and discovered, "I absolutely loved performing." The teacher clearly knew how to pick a star!

After his early success, Louis wanted to take it further, and auditioned for *The X Factor*. He had his first try in 2009, and made it through in 2010. "When I tried out the second time, I was more driven than ever," he told *J-14*, though he "really struggled" during the boot-camp phase. But he always felt encouraged by the talent around him. "I even had a photo taken with Harry because I knew he was going to be famous." Turns out the teacher wasn't the only one with good instincts. Now text us that pic, please!

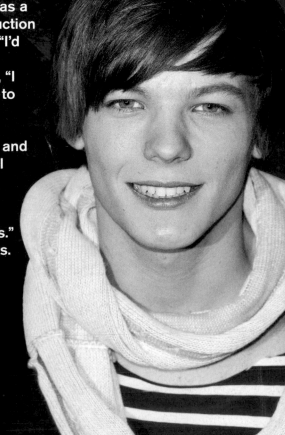

"We came from nothing and had no experience as a group at all. By the time we came to the end of [*The X Factor*], we were a completely different group. We worked so hard and achieved so much. We also became really close mates—we're just all so grateful that we got along so well from the start."

— LOUIS, THEHOTHITS.COM

FRIENDS IN HIGH SCHOOL PLACES

From the age of 4, Adele Laurie Blue Adkins loved to sing. The only child of a single mom (her parents divorced when she was 3), she remembers giving little concerts in her room for her mother, who would gather together all the lamps and shine them on her daughter to make a spotlight.

At 14, Adele won admission to the prestigious BRIT School for Performing Arts & Technology. While at BRIT, Adele came into her own as an artist. She almost didn't make it through because she was always late to everything. Her chronic lateness came to a head when she was one of 20 students chosen to perform at a music festival and she missed it. "It was pretty horrible. I almost did get kicked out of the school for that," she told *Rolling Stone.*

Just before graduation, while Adele was planning her 18th birthday, she told *Cosmopolitan,* she got a strange email, supposedly from someone who worked at a music label and wanted to meet her. Earlier, a school friend had set up a Myspace page with her songs. "I thought it was just some [nut] on the Internet so I emailed back and said 'Leave me alone, I'm organizing my birthday party.' Still, when her mystery correspondent replied, asking if she'd been signed, she told him no and said he could contact her again after she graduated. Lucky thing she relented, because the guy turned out to be an executive from XL Recordings, the British label that represents megastars Radiohead and M.I.A. When Adele checked him out, she was stunned. "We met; they liked me and signed me," she told *Cosmopolitan.* "I feel bad telling that story because it was really that easy."

Adele back in 2008

"I've never wanted to look like models on the covers of magazines. I represent the majority of women, and I'm very proud of that." —PEOPLE

19...

Getting signed to a record label was one thing, but coming up with songs for a whole album—yikes! Adele had a few songs, like "Hometown Glory," which she wrote when she was 16, but an album requires 10 to 12 songs. "I've always liked writing songs," she told *Cosmopolitan*. "But when I suddenly had to, I was dry and couldn't come up with anything. I was very nervous because I thought the label would say I wasn't ready."

Then fate stepped in. Adele was in her first serious romantic relationship at the time and her boyfriend cheated on her. She told *Glamour*, "Rather than being extremely mopey, I managed to write songs. Which kind of eased the pain." The result was Adele's 2008 debut album, *19.* The first single, "Chasing Pavements," was huge. *Billboard* wrote, "Adele truly has potential to become among the most respected and inspiring international artists of her generation."

The music bible may be on to something. At the 2008 Grammys, she won "Best Female Pop Vocal Performance," for "Chasing Pavements" and was also named "Best New Artist."

ADELE'S INSPIRATIONS

During Adele's first year at BRIT, Amy Winehouse took the music world by storm. "Amy Winehouse came out with her first album," Adele told *Cosmopolitan*. "It was amazing. It's my favorite." Adele looks up to other female artists as well. My favorite singers are Etta James and Aretha Franklin," she told *Cosmopolitan*, "If you were to look up the word *singer* in the dictionary, you'd see their names." Adele has added Beyoncé to that list. "She's been a huge and constant part of my life as an artist since I was about 10 or 11," Adele told *Vogue.* "I love how all her songs are about empowerment."

After Adele zoomed to the top of the charts with *19,* she hardly took a breath before she was working on her follow-up album. Her first effort had brought her fame and a U.S. record label, Columbia. Then came the pressure to meet everyone's expectations for the second album. She was surrounded by ideas, plans, and suggestions, but Adele knew she had to rely on her instincts again. Coincidentally, her love life once again came to the rescue. "It was my first grown-up, intense relationship," she told *People.* But it, too, resulted in a split just as she was ready to write songs for her album. "We broke up mutually, and I was desperate to write about it," Adele told *Rolling Stone,* "'cause I can't talk about my feelings to anyone. To my mum, to my therapist, to friends, to myself in the mirror—I can't really do it. I've always written down how I feel."

The results of her heartbreak included songs such as "Rolling in the Deep," "Set Fire to the Rain," and "Turning Tables." But the song that embodied all the hurt and tears was "Someone Like You." "Even now I get emotional performing that," Adele told *Cosmopolitan.* "It was very scary because it was such an honest thing for me to write. I don't think I'll ever write a better song than that. I think that'll be my song, you know?"

In late 2011, Adele met fellow Brit, Simon Konecki, 37, who runs the charity Drop4Drop, which provides potable drinking water for developing countries. Their relationship is serious, though she can be far from serious at times: She nicknamed Simon "Waterboy," in reference to his charity. They got engaged and shortly after announced Adele was pregnant. Adele and Simon welcomed their baby boy into the world on October 21, 2012.

THE VOICE

Fate had more in store for Adele—both bad and good. Beginning in January 2011, just as Adele was heading out for the promotional tour for *21*, her voice gave out. "That day it just went while I was onstage in Paris during a radio show. It was literally like someone had pulled a curtain over it." She needed surgery and four months in silence to heal her vocal-cords and avoid ruining her extraordinary voice. So she changed her hectic life. She told *Vogue,* "I think I just needed to be silenced. And when you are silent, everyone else around you is silent. The noise in my life just stopped. It was like I was floating in the sea...It was brilliant. It was my body telling me to fix me.

I had so much time to kind of go over things and get over things, which is amazing."

Five months after her vocal chord surgery she made her first live appearance at the February 2011 Grammys, singing "Rolling in the Deep." The audience gave her a standing ovation. That night Adele took home six Grammys: "Record of the Year" for "Rolling in the Deep," "Album of the Year" for *21,* "Song of the Year" for "Rolling in the Deep," "Best Pop Solo Performance" for "Someone Like You," "Best Pop Vocal Album" for *21, and* "Best Short Form Music Video" for "Rolling in the Deep."

CONOR MAYNARD

NO TIME TO EAT

Even before he could form words, Brit-boy Conor Maynard was singing the praises of music. When he was just learning to talk, he told scholastic.com "I'd go, 'Zic on. Zic on,' and I meant I wanted to hear music. And then once my auntie was looking after me, and I was going, 'Zic on. Zic on,' and she thought I was going to be sick… Then my mom got there and she was like, 'No, he just wants to listen to music.'"

When he was older and going to school, he would head home after the last bell to write songs and make music videos in his bedroom. Today, those videos are part of Conor's YouTube collection, but back then, it was all just for fun. Then something happened. Friends noticed that Conor was really talented. "There was this one day…when I was walking down the road after school, and I was singing to myself and messing about with my friends," he told *The Telegraph*. "An older girl from school turned around and said, 'Boy, you can sing!'"

Soon, friends and friends of friends were requesting that Conor sing for them. It became a regular thing. Soon he was doing daily lunchtime concerts at school. Then he put up some of his homemade videos on YouTube, creating them from "two Singstar microphones from Playstation 2, taped to my bedpost." He didn't start posting to YouTube in hopes that he'd get famous—it was, "mainly so I'd get to eat my lunch at school rather than having to sing all through my break!"

IT'S NOT EASY BEING CLEAN

Conor is the first to admit he isn't known for a tidy room—it was true before, and it's true now. Even when he filmed his videos, he didn't bother with the set. It makes his mom freak. "I never give my room a tidy before filming," he told firtsnews.com.uk, "My mum has actually told me off regarding the state of my room in a few videos!"

"I can see why [I'm compared with Justin Bieber]— we're both young and came through YouTube. But I don't like being boxed in. I would much rather people listened to the album and made up their own mind rather than being told what it is...I named the album *Contrast* because I wanted to show it wasn't a Bieber 2.0 album." **— THE GUARDIAN**

FUN FACTS!

» Conor's fave celebrity crush is Megan Fox. He says it's too bad that she's married.

» For him, the perfect date is just laughing a lot and getting to know each other in a quiet setting.

» As a little kid he said all his S's like Z's and would tell his mom that he was too "zick" to go to school.

» He says that his favorite male musical artist is Ed Sheeran.

» Conor's music reflects a heavy rap influence, but he says he is a huge fan of rock groups like Good Charlotte and Green Day.

NE-YO CALLING

Conor's fan base expanded once he started posting covers of songs like Usher's "OMG" and Ne-Yo's "Beautiful Monster," which earned more than a million YouTube views. And then Conor got a phone call from Ne-Yo's manager, who told him the R&B phenom wanted to mentor him. Conor told mtvnews.com, "I remember when I first got the phone call…I was like, 'OK, I want to believe this. [But] it's a bit shady.' I just didn't want to get out to America and then, you know, have one of my friends calling from my hometown go, 'It was me—gotcha!' So I had to make sure. Sure enough, I was sitting on Skype with Ne-Yo about 1:30 a.m. talking about music and him wanting to sign me. That's what started this massive buzz in the U.K." The R&B superstar invited Conor to meet him in Los Angeles—and go into the studio with him! Soon Conor had a record deal, working with Ne-Yo and music producer Pharrell Williams. Conor spent time with Williams at his Miami studio working on his debut album, *Contrast*.

"That was an insane time," Conor told *Billboard.* In an interview with MTV News he elaborated. "I got to work with some incredible people. There are some amazing, amazing names I'm honored to have on this album." The experience was kind of overwhelming. "I had to control myself [and] not want to run in there and lick their faces…I had to be normal…It was exciting and it made me very, very driven to want to prove myself to them."

OLLY MURS

SEMI-PRO GOES POP!

Few people who knew Olly Murs growing up in Witham, Essex, U.K., could have guessed he would become a pop star. He was more into sports and was the star center on his Notley High School football team—that's soccer to us Yanks! Olly went on to play semiprofessional football for th Witham Town team, but had to give it up when he was injured. After he'd recovered and spent a head-clearing three months in Australia backpacking, he returned home and went to a Justin Timberlake concert.

Olly back in 2009

"I was blown away by how talented he was," e told *Maximum Pop!* The experience left Olly spiring "to perform like him one day."

Olly was finally okay with shelving his otball dreams, and decided he'd try to make in show business. His first move was to udition for the sixth season of *The X Factor*. e immediately won over hard-to-please judge mon Cowell, who put him right through as contestant. Week after week Olly wowed e judges and even began throwing in some nce moves, like his trademark "Olly Wiggle."

Although he lost to singer Joe McElderry, Simon gave Olly a record deal with his label, Syco, and released two U.K. albums: *Olly Murs* and *In Case You Didn't Know*. He also became good friends with those other *X Factor* non-winners—One Direction! Olly toured the U.S. with 1D in 2012 as the lads' opening act. Olly told *Popstar!*, "In Detroit, Louie and Liam came running out with Nerf guns and they were hitting me in the back of the head with plastic guns throughout my sound check." But no hard feelings. "They're just great guys."

RIGHT PLACE, RIGHT TIME ——

Olly now has over two million followers on Twitter, and he's about to explode in the States. He says that making it this far is all due to his effort and dedication—from *The X Factor* forward. Olly knows there's no such thing as overnight success, so he's working it. But that just makes him more determined. He spent the fall of 2012 promoting and touring for his third album, *Right Time, Right Place,* and working on an illustrated autobiography, *Happy Days,* due in 2013. He may someday merchandise replicas of the porkpie hat he calls his "trophy" hat and wears in almost every show. He didn't mean for it to become his trademark look, he says. It's just that wearing the hat gives him 45 minutes extra to sleep in the morning because it lets him skip working on his hair. No need if it's covered up!

SOUNDTRACK BY OLLY

Most of the songs that have carried Olly to success are inspired by real events in his life—and, continuing in the tradition of Taylor Swift and Adele, he often draws from heartbreak. Romance gone sour—and remembering the good times—is the subject of his U.S. debut single, "Heart Skips a Beat," from his third album, *Right Place, Right Time*. "Whenever you're in a relationship, you have that favorite song that reminds you of when you

first got together or when you first kissed," he told seventeen.com. "It's about that feeling you have when...you listen to the song that you used to dance to with that person."

"Heart Skips a Beat" may be just that song for a lot of couples who are getting together right now. But that's kind of sad. We prefer to think that someone, somewhere, is getting their party on to Olly's "Dance with Me Tonight."

LIAM HEMSWORTH

Liam with his parents and brother, Chris, opening night, season five, for the Australian Dancing with the Stars, September, 2006

THE HOTTIE FROM DOWN UNDER

With his incredible good looks and considerable talent you might think Liam Hemsworth would have an easy time making it in Hollywood. But nothing is easy in Hollywood!

Liam's big acting breaks in his native Australia came on a kid's show and later on a popular soap opera. But it was Liam's older, actor brother, Chris, who helped pave the way for his baby brother in the U.S. Chris moved here first and Liam was set to follow. Liam had won a role in the film *The Expendables,* via a taped script reading. Everything was a go until his role was cut. Shortly after hearing that bad news, Liam was asked to test for the lead role in *Thor.* He flew right over and moved into Chris's small West Hollywood apartment. Nothing was going to stop Liam! Well, one thing did put a snag in his road to stardom. He was up against several other actors for *Thor* and he lost out to one of them...his brother Chris.

Liam's attitude: No worries, mate! Good thing he was keeping his chin up, because he went on to lose several more roles. He told *Men's Health,* "I had a bunch of films one year, four or five, that were supposed to happen that never ended up happening. It's kind of the nature of the business." But you can't lose 'em all! Liam was cast in *The Last Song, Expendables 2,* and most notably, 2012's *The Hunger Games,* the movie that made him a superstar.

"I grew up on an island in Australia—Phillip Island—so I surf as much as I can. I'm trying to get down to the beach. Surfing is great because you can clear your head and get away from all the attention and that kind of thing."

— *LIFE STORY*

SEEING STARS

To prepare for his *Hunger Games* character, Gale, Liam went on intense nutritional and workout programs. His challenge was to lose weight and muscle mass without endangering his health. "I lost quite a bit of weight for the role," he told *Men's Health.* "My character lives in [impoverished] District 12 in the film....He's hunting for his food every day and trying to provide for himself and his family."

Liam lost the weight, maintained his health, and became one of the most sought-after actors in Hollywood after *The Hunger Games.* That presents a challenge for him, too: he says he prefers staying out of the spotlight, but starring in a string of films makes that pretty hard. It still amazes him when he's stopped on the street and asked for an autograph. But he's getting used to it. He told *Men's Health,* "It hasn't got too crazy at this point. I'm still able to do normal things. I can go places, and it doesn't get too crazy. We'll see how it is in five years." We can't predict what will happen in five years, but we do know that over the next few years, fans can look forward to Liam in *The Hunger Games: Catching Fire, Paranoia, Timeless, Empire State* and *Arabian Nights.*

CODY SIMPSON

FOLLOW YOUR HEART

Cody Simpson was not one of the cool kids at school when he was growing up on Australia's Gold Coast. "It wasn't like I was…captain of the rugby team or something," he told *Twist*. Swimming was more his style. "I would mostly be in the water or I'd be in the music room with my music teacher. Guys would tease me because I was into music."

The teasing didn't stop Cody from doing what he liked. He was smart enough to be true to himself and after awhile his schoolmates' jibes no longer bothered him. Cody told *Twist*, "I think it's always good not to follow the cool thing to do. It's

good to go on your own path and do what you like not what everyone else does."

If you think your own path revolves around music, Cody recommends that you use social media to get noticed. "I think YouTube is a great way to do it," he told seventeen.com. "Just work hard at it. If it's your dream, then it'll come. But have fun with it as well."

Of course, it always helps to have a family who totally supports your dreams. Once it became obvious that Cody was committed to his music and that executives in the music business were interested in him, his parents, Brad and Angie,

Cody back in 2007

made a major decision and moved their
family—Cody, younger sister, Alli, and
younger brother, Tom—halfway around the
world. In 2010 the Simpsons left Australia
to make a home in Los Angeles.

Cody has said in interviews that the
most difficult thing he has ever done
was to ask his family to move to L.A. for
his career. He admitted that the huge
change took some getting used to. Now
he loves the people, the sunshine, and
beach, as well as all the show business
opportunities.

Q: How did you get the idea to start putting your songs on YouTube?

A: Well, I did a concert. I performed "I'm Yours" by Jason Mraz with a girl and she wanted me to put it up on YouTube, so that was my very first video. And then a few people started liking it, so I put more covers of artists that inspired me, like Justin Timberlake. And more people started liking those....so that's when I got a call from a producer.

— SCHOLASTIC.COM

108

PARADISE FOUND! ——

Cody had a big hit with his first single, "IYIYI," which featured Flo Rida, and he scored again with his next single, "Summertime." He followed those with two EPs—*4U* in 2010 and *Coast to Coast* in 2011. After that he split his time among touring, making appearances, and working on his first full-length album, *Paradise*, which went on sale in the fall of 2012.

Paradise is Cody's pride and joy. The promotional blitz that accompanied its release included *Finding Cody,* a film shown exclusively on Warner Music Group's YouTube channel, The Warner Sound. Cody spent last summer touring with Big Time Rush, and even found himself onstage with Justin Bieber and Carly Rae Jepsen for a few shows. These performances were great practice for Cody's future headlining dates!

Cody has always kept both feet on the ground despite great success in the musical world. He told Ryan Seacrest in an 102.7 KIIS FM interview that while he's not doing laundry these days, he does have other chores to do at home. "When I am home…I do the dishwasher and all that stuff. I was really hyped yesterday morning 'cause my album had just dropped and it was doing really well on iTunes and then my mom goes, 'Cody, do the washing and I was like, 'This is not 'paradise.'"

Whoosh! Back to reality! But you can believe that as he was loading the family dishwasher, he was smiling from ear to ear!

SUPERSTAR MUTUAL ADMIRATION SOCIETY

You know you've made it when fellow teen superstars say they're fans. After spending time with Justin Bieber and Selena Gomez, Cody said, "Selena was…telling me that she was a fan of mine. It was supercool for a fellow young star to be supportive, and I'm a big fan of hers as well. Justin is cool—I was hanging out with him. He's a really nice guy. He's real supportive of what I do." — *J-14*

First Steps

TEAM DISNEY, TEAM NICK, or TEAM BARNEY

Many of your favorite celebs began their journey to stardom on one of these three paths!

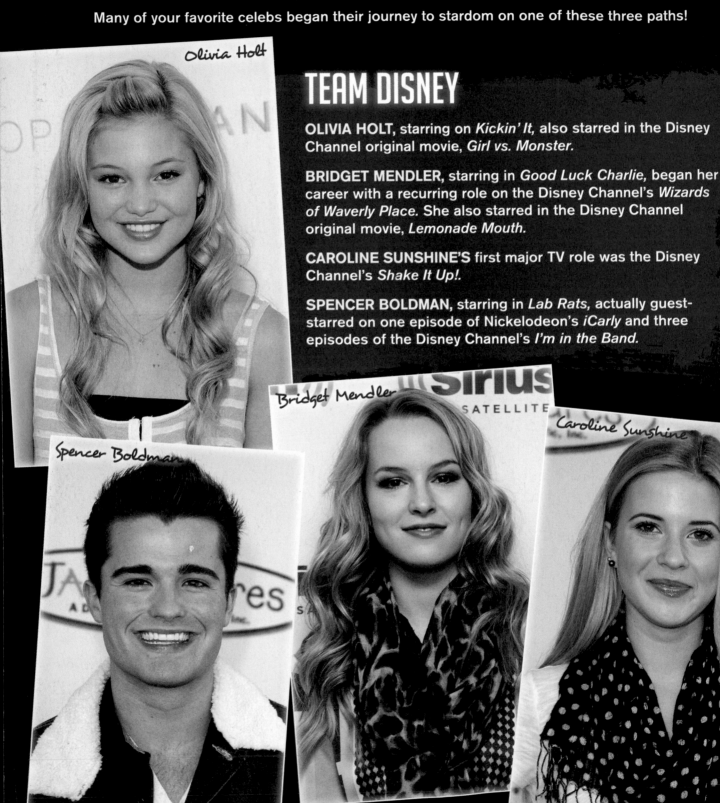

TEAM DISNEY

OLIVIA HOLT, starring on *Kickin' It,* also starred in the Disney Channel original movie, *Girl vs. Monster.*

BRIDGET MENDLER, starring in *Good Luck Charlie,* began her career with a recurring role on the Disney Channel's *Wizards of Waverly Place.* She also starred in the Disney Channel original movie, *Lemonade Mouth.*

CAROLINE SUNSHINE'S first major TV role was the Disney Channel's *Shake It Up!.*

SPENCER BOLDMAN, starring in *Lab Rats,* actually guest-starred on one episode of Nickelodeon's *iCarly* and three episodes of the Disney Channel's *I'm in the Band.*

Olivia Holt

Bridget Mendler

Caroline Sunshine

Spencer Boldman

TEAM NICKELODEON

JAKE T. AUSTIN, best known for starring in the Disney Channel's *Wizards of Waverly Place*, got his start on Nickelodeon as the voice of Diego on *Dora The Explorer* and *Go, Diego, Go!*.

MIRANDA COSGROVE, famous as the star of *iCarly*, got her start on *Drake & Josh*.

ASHLEY ARGOTA, starring on *Bucket & Skinner's Epic Adventures*, got her start on *True Jackson, VP*.

ARIANA GRANDE, costarred with Victoria Justice on *Victorious*, and currently stars in the *Victorious* spin-off, *Sam & Cat*.

Miranda Cosgrove

Jake T. Austin

Debby Ryan

TEAM BARNEY

DEBBY RYAN began her career on *Barney & Friends* and *Barney: Let's Go to the Firehouse* before she switched teams to the Disney Channel and costarred in *The Suite Life on Deck*. Now she has her own Disney Channel series, *Jessie*.

SELENA GOMEZ, a sparkling Disney Channel star of *Wizards of Waverly Place*, actually got her start on *Barney & Friends*!

DEMI LOVATO got her big break on the Disney Channel's *Sonny with A Chance*, but her real start was on *Barney & Friends*, along with her pal Selena Gomez!

Demi Lovato

All Hail to the King

Michael Jackson wanted to be known as The King of Pop, and almost four years after he died, millions of his mulitgenerational fans around the world are still happy to honor him with that title. Among Michael's achievements were seven multiplatinum albums, thirteen number one singles in the U.S., and recognition by Guinness World Records as the most successful entertainer of all time. He has also been a major inspiration to many of today's top artists and performers. Here's what some of them have said about their idol:

MADONNA:

He was the king who inspired us all....I don't know what artist wasn't inspired by him. Everybody grew up in awe of him. (Interview with Ryan Seacrest)

JAY-Z:

My favorite [Michael Jackson] album is *Off the Wall*...[It] was timeless. It didn't have a genre. It was colorless. It was ageless. The whole family could listen to it. The album had huge records. They were so emotional!" (singersroom.com)

JUSTIN TIMBERLAKE:

He has been an inspiration to multiple generations, and I will always cherish the moments I shared with him onstage and all of the things I learned about music from him and the time we spent together. (*People*)

BEYONCÉ:

My first producer used to make me listen to Michael Jackson's live performance of 'Who's Loving You.' For whatever reason he could evoke more emotion than an adult. Michael taught me that sometimes you have to forget technique, forget what you have on. If you feel silly, you have to go from the gut, just let it go. Michael Jackson changed me and helped me to become the artist I am. Thank you, Michael. (*Rolling Stone*)

USHER:

[Michael Jackson] influenced me in so many ways, more than just music…as a humanitarian, as a philanthropist, as an artist, as an individual who transcended culture. I wouldn't be who I am today without Michael Jackson. They say if you ever want to be great, you've got to study who the greats studied, so, of course, I studied his moves—studied them down to a T…I consider myself very fortunate to have had the opportunity to share the stage with him, to know him personally, and I am always going to remember him. (MTV News)

All Hail to the King
THE NEXT GENERATION

NE-YO:

I was submitting songs to [Michael Jackson]. I was writing songs, demoing them, and sending them to him for him to critique. There were about 10 songs that he had picked that he was going to record. We stopped because he started getting ready for his tour....What I definitely learned from Michael Jackson is that simple is always better. As a songwriter, as an artist—period. (virgin.com)

DRAKE:

He was young and had the world excited and anticipating his every move. [My song, "Over,"] was my homage to him and the impact that he had on the world that I live in. (MTV News)

ED SHEERAN:

"The most influential artist of the past 25 years has been Michael Jackson. I think there are a lot of people who have taken influence from what he's done and how he's kind of gone about things." (fhm.com)

JUSTIN BIEBER: ⎯⎯⎯⎯

Every time that I go out onstage, every time I go out and perform, I'm always trying to be the best and that's what [Michael] always did....I basically released my first single the week he passed, so it was really unfortunate....That was one person I really wanted to meet. (*Digital Spy*)

JAMES MASLOW: ⎯⎯⎯⎯

I don't think there's one person who wouldn't want to [have shared] a stage with [Michael Jackson]. He was absolutely the best entertainer in the world. From dancing to singing to capturing the crowd, he literally gave his life doing that." (scholastic.com)

Home Sweet Home

NAME THE CITY AND THE CELEB

How well do you know the hometowns of your favorite celebs? Below, we've given you hints for 10 of them. Some of the clues are really easy. Others are so tricky you'll probably need to do some research! Once you have figured out the correct cities, match the superstar with his or her hometown. Good luck!

1 This Canadian city is known for its active arts community. The Avon Theatre is home to many of these events. It's also where your fave played his guitar and sang on the theater's steps.

CELEB:

CITY:

2 This California city is home to beautiful Spanish architecture. One popular tourist attraction, built in 1786, is known as "Queen of the Missions."

CELEB:

CITY:

3 This is the largest city in Kansas and is the hometown of comic strip character Dennis the Menace.

CELEB:

CITY:

4 This bling-bling California city is known for its celebrity residents, zip code (90210), and luxurious shopping strip (Rodeo Drive). It is also the setting for the film and TV series *Clueless*.

CELEB:

CITY:

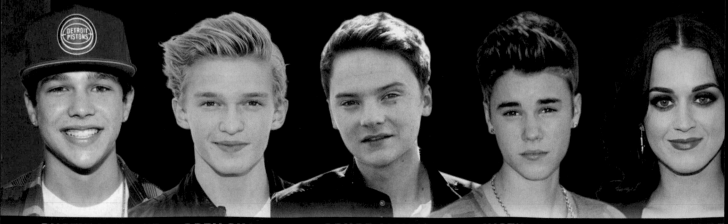

AUSTIN MAHONE   CODY SIMPSON   CONOR MAYNARD   JUSTIN BIEBER   KATY PERR

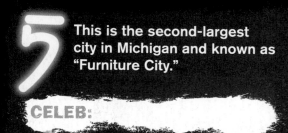

5
This is the second-largest city in Michigan and known as "Furniture City."

CELEB:

CITY:

6
This city's nickname is the "Big Apple."

CELEB:

CITY:

7
This is one of England's most popular seaside resorts, known for its beaches and health spas. Jane Austen used it as a location for part of her book *Pride and Prejudice*.

CELEB:

CITY:

8
This city in Queensland, Australia, is the location of a popular get-away called Surfer's Paradise. It is also the original home of Aussies Kylie and Danni Minogue.

CELEB:

CITY:

9
This British West Midlands town's nickname for its residents is "Wulfrians" or "Yam Yams."

CELEB:

CITY:

10
This Texas town is home to the historic army fort, the Alamo.

CELEB:

CITY:

1. Justin Bieber—Stratford, Ontario; 2. Katy Perry—Santa Barbara, CA; 3. BTR's Kendall Schmidt—Wichita, KS; 4. Logan Lerman—Beverly Hills, CA; 5. Taylor Lautner—Grand Rapids, MI; 6. Lady Gaga—New York, NY; 7. Conor Maynard—Brighton, England; 8. Cody Simpson—Gold Coast, Australia; 9. Liam Payne—Wolverhampton, England; 10. Austin Mahone—San Antonio, TX

KENDALL SCHMIDT   LADY GAGA   LIAM PAYNE   LOGAN LERMAN   TAYLOR LAUTNER

Find 'Em!

CELEBS AND THEIR MENTORS

Achieving success is never a one-man (or one-woman) operation. The superstars you love to watch and listen to became famous by working hard, but they've also had help from others who came before them. These mentors have encouraged, challenged, and advised your faves as they've developed their careers. Hidden in the puzzle box at the right are the names of the following stars connected to the names of their mentors. Can you find them?

JUSTIN BIEBER

CONOR MAYNARD

DRAKE

JADEN SMITH

RACHEL CROW

NICKI MINAJ

Remember, the names can run vertically, horizontally, diagonally, forward, and backward!

```
J B M T S I M O N C O W E L L
U S H E R T I N V R O L I T V
S O L T N U I V O R L J N M B
T R A E W Y C B C R Y U C C V
I D R A K E A L Y U I G J O F
N C E B T Y E W B M T A J N K
B G I E W H T Y L D N A S O V
I N D L C O P X C I D W G R H
E C A A Y I B U M E L N N M I
B O R P E R S I N D G Y E A H
E N I O P E K S C Q S H I Y H
R J V O D C M P L E E Z R N O
T I B B I I F Y U N K O C A Z
X Y C N T W E K B L T I E R Z
    I H T I M S L L I W T N
```

```
N D Z M I L L S M I T H Q S
Z R E I T L B K E W T N C Y X
Z A C O K N U Y F I I B B I T
N R Z E E L P M C D O V J R
H Y I H S Q C S K E P O I N E
H A E Y G D N I S R E P R O B
I M N N L E M U B I Y A A C E
H R G W D I C X P O C L D N I
V O S A N D L Y T H W E I G B
K N J A T M B W E Y T B E C N
F O J G I U Y L A E K A R D J
V C C U Y R C B Y W E A R T
B M J L R O V I U N T L O S
V T I L O R V N I T R E H S U
L L E W O C N O M I S T M B J
```

119

Lights! Camera! Action!

FASCINATING FIRSTS OF YOUR FAVES

Do you know the back stories of the superstars? Do you remember that Justin first officially toured on the *Urban Behavior Tour* in 2009? Would you be able to name his first big acting gig? It was *CSI: Crime Scene Investigation;* he did his first episode in 2010 and his second a year later…just in case you drew a blank!

    This test will separate the superstar fans— from the *supernova* superstar fans! Ready?

1 Lucas Cruikshank guest-starred on several TV sitcoms. Which was the first?

HANNAH MONTANA

CARLY

SUPAH NINJAS

2 Liam Hemsworth appeared on some of Australian TV's most popular series. What was the first in which he was a recurring character?

NEIGHBOURS

HOME AND AWAY

THE ELEPHANT PRINCESS

3 Selena Gomez made her jump into the big time as Alex Russo on *Wizards of Waverly Place.* On what Disney Channel series did she first guest star?

THE SUITE LIFE OF ZACH & CODY

HANNAH MONTANA

THE SUITE LIFE ON DECK

4 Taylor Swift's concert tour began in 2009 and ended in 2010. What was the name of the tour?

RED TOUR

SPEAK NOW WORLD TOUR

FEARLESS TOUR

5

Ne-Yo released his first album, *In My Own Words*, in 2006. Which single from the album was the first to hit number one on the *Billboard Top 100*?

"STAY"

"WHEN YOU'RE MAD"

"SO SICK"

6

Drake, who was born Aubrey Drake Graham, started out as an actor. What was the name of the TV series on which he was a regular character?

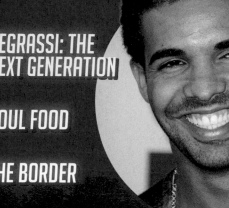

DEGRASSI: THE NEXT GENERATION

SOUL FOOD

THE BORDER

7

Rachel Crow, who grabbed the world's attention on the U.S. version of *The X Factor*, released her first single in 2012. What was it called?

"LEMONADE"

"MEAN GIRLS"

"MY KIND OF WONDERFUL"

8

Taylor Lautner's first starring role was in a 2005 movie. What was the name of the movie and of his character?

VALENTINE'S DAY AS WILLY

CHEAPER BY THE DOZEN 2 AS ELIOT

THE ADVENTURES OF SHARKBOY AND LAVAGIRL 3-D AS SHARKBOY

1. *iCarly* in 2009, 2. *Neighbours* in 2008, 3. *The Suite Life of Zach & Cody* in 2006, 4. Fearless Tour; 5. "So Sick"; 6. *Degrassi: The Next Generation* in 2001–2009, 7. "Mean Girls"; 8. *The Adventures of Sharkboy and Lavagirl 3-D* as Sharkboy

School Days

Your favorite superstars have brilliant careers now, but they started out like everyone else—as kids going to school! And just like you, they had good times, bad times, and just plain funny moments!

ROSHON FEGAN: OOPS!

"I started to play football in middle school," *Shake It Up!'s* Roshon told *Twist.* "I'm a little guy, so when the coach threw me the ball from all the way across the field, I was running super fast, thinking, 'I'm gonna catch this!' but I wasn't sure how! So I try to catch it, but it goes straight through my hands and hits me dead in the center of my nose! It was embarrassing because I was surrounded by big jocks who saw it happen!"

JAMES MASLOW: SCHOOL VS SURF

"When I was in high school in Coronado, CA, we had open lunch, so you could leave for lunch," Big Time Rush's James told *J-14.* "Every once in a while I wouldn't come back to school because I'd go surfing or something! The teachers definitely didn't appreciate that … [then they would give me] extra homework and detention!"

KEKE PALMER: WORDS CAN HURT

"I got teased in elementary school," Keke told *Twist.* "It wa hard—they just didn't like me. They didn't like the way I talked…I sounded different than they did. They were mor proper-sounding, but I used a lot of slang. They didn't understand much about me. Still, I kept trying. I would jus try to be nice back to them."

CODY SIMPSON: FIRST-DAY FREAKOUTS

"When I was younger, I never wanted to leave my mom!" Cody told *Twist*. "Every first day of school, I'd just cry. I'd hold on to her and rip her shirt to try not to leave her! Mom would get upset because I was hysterical, and it was horrible. I still remember. But then afterward I'd be on the playground having the best time."

ARIANA GRANDE: MEAN GIRLS—WHO CARES?

"I was always teased," *Sam & Cat*'s Ariana told *Bop*. "You just have to know that you're a cool person. Be proud of yourself and be like, 'Hey, this is who I am!'"

DAREN KAGASOFF: BUZZ LIGHTYEAR!

I had just gotten my hair buzzed and I stepped on the bus," *Secret Life*'s Daren told *M* about n embarrassing moment in elementary school. My friend said, You look like Buzz ightyear!' I never haved my head gain. I have big ars—it just doesn't vork for me."

RACHEL CROW: BACK-TO-SCHOOL SHOPPING

What's Rachel's favorite thing about school? "We'll plan a day the summer and we'll go to Walmart and buy all our school upplies and cool books," Rachel told *Twist*. "Then we buy our utfits. Then on the first day, we take a picture! It's really nice."

Fan-demonium

SORT IT OUT!

Here's a fun game for true fans. Listed below are the names of eight favorite musical celebrities. Below their names are word scrambles for the nicknames they've given their fans. Some are easy, some are hard…all are fun to unscramble!

ONE DIRECTION
CTIEORINDERS

JUSTIN BIEBER
RSBELEIBE

LADY GAGA
TTILLE NSOTERMS

CONOR MAYNARD
CNYISAMA

KATY PERRY
YCTAATSK

NICKI MINAJ
BZRAB

> "I've said it before and I will say it forever —
> **I HAVE THE BEST FANS IN THE WORLD!**"
> — DEMI LOVATO, SEVENTEEN.COM

TAYLOR SWIFT
ESSWIIFT

DEMI LOVATO
VATIOCSL

ONE DIRECTION: Directioners; JUSTIN BIEBER: Beliebers; LADY GAGA: Little Monsters; CONOR MAYNARD: Mayniacs; KATY PERRY: Katycats; NICKI MINAJ: Barbz; TAYLOR SWIFT: Swifties; DEMI LOVATO: Lovatics

Cool Stuff to Know

SHARE WITH YOUR FRIENDS!

KATY PERRY: IN MOTION

On Katy's *California Dreams Tour* she made 15 costume changes during the two-hour show—believe it or not, she changed eight times during one song!

CODY CRUSH

Cody Simpson wrote his second song, "Ride My Rollercoaster," about a crush. "I was 10, and I had a crush on this girl, who was, like, 12 or 13. She thought I was cute and young, and I sang for her." – *Teen Vogue*

DRIVE CAREFULLY IN BEVERLY HILLS

JUSTIN BIEBER: THE BEST HE CAN BE

"I am a natural competitor. I am a hockey player, basketball player, and soccer player. I was known as an athlete back at my school in Stratford when I was younger and I like to compete....I want to be the best. That trait can be annoying, especially when it comes to Ping-Pong™. If you want to play, bring it on!" – *Justin Bieber: Just Getting Started*

HOW NICKI MINAJ CHILLS

To unwind after a crazy day, "I watch *Judge Judy!*" —*Cosmopolitan*

GAGA'S YEARBOOK

This was printed under her picture in the senior yearbook of Stefani Germanotta—now known as Lady Gaga.

NAME: Stefani Joanne Germanotta

NICKNAME: Stefi, The germ

USUALLY SEEN: Singing

PICTURE HER: Without her midriff showing

DREAM: Headlining at Madison Square Garden

SEPARATED AT BIRTH: Britney Spears

PRIZED POSSESSION: Her piano

PET PEEVE: "Ordinary" people

KENDALL SCHMIDT: HOMEWORK HAZE

"I was a big slacker. I put off schoolwork until the last minute. The subject I disliked the most was math. It was just too much." However, for his fans, Kendall has some advice. "Get to work, because school is your first task that you have to finish, and then you can do whatever you want." — *Bop*

LIAM HEMSWORTH: UNIQUE STYLE

A reporter doing an interview with Liam noticed he had a fuchsia iPhone case. He laughed and said, "Thank you for noticing. I had a leather one, but it fell apart. I found this one at home. Yes, I have a pink iPhone. And, yes, my friends make fun of me!" — *InStyle*

Photo Credits

2: Mike Stobe/Getty Images (Bieber circle), Kevin Winter/Getty Images (Bieber rectangle, Ne-Yo circle), AP Photo/Mark Humphrey (Swift circle), Kevin Mazur/WireImage/Getty Images (Swfit Rectangle), Mike Marsland/WireImage/Getty Images (Ne-Yo rectangle). 3: Chris Polk/FilmMagic/Getty Images (Perry circle), Chris McGrath/Getty Images (Perry rectangle). 6: Alberto E. Rodriguez/Getty Images for KCA (Big Time Rush), Christopher Polk/Getty Images for Clear Channel (Swift), Mike Marsland/WireImage/Getty Images (Ne-yo), Steven Lawton/FilmMagic/Getty Images (Bieber), Kevin Mazur/WireImage/Getty Images (Minaj), Jeff Fusco/Getty Images (Jepsen), Stephen M. Dowell/Orlando Sentinel/MCT via Getty Images (One Direction). 8: Mike Stobe/Getty Images. 9: George Pimentel/WireImage/Getty Images. 10–11: Virginia Sherwood/NBC/NBCU Photo Bank via Getty Images. 10: Larry Busacca/Getty Images for NARAS. 12: Kevin Mazur/WireImage/Getty Images (with team), Kevin Winter/Getty Images (on stage). 13: Steven Lawton/FilmMagic/Getty Images. 14: Chelsea Lauren/WireImage/Getty Images. 15: Mark Davis/WireImage/Getty Images. 16–17: Jeff Fusco/Getty Images. 16: Virginia Sherwood/NBC/NBCU Photo Bank via Getty Images. 18: Bryan Steffy/Getty Images. 19: Christopher Polk/WireImage/Getty Images (with Braun), Paul Drinkwater/NBC/NBCU Photo Bank via Getty Images (Jepsen). 20: Vera Anderson/WireImage/Getty Images. 21: Gilbert Carrasquillo/Getty Images (with dad), Alberto E. Rodriguez/Getty Images (Smith). 22: AP Photo/Mark Humphrey. 23: Michael Buckner/Getty Images. 24–25: Michael Buckner/Getty Images. 24: Jason Merritt/Getty Images. 26: Isaac Brekken/Getty Images for Clear Channel. 27: Kevin Mazur/WireImage/Getty Images (with mic), Christopher Polk/Getty Images for Clear Channel (arm out). 28: Larry Marano/Getty Images (playing pool), Jeff Schear/Getty Images for Kellogg's Pop Tarts (red hat). 29: C Flanigan/WireImage/Getty Images. 30: Ray Tamarra/Getty Images. 31: Kevin Mazur/WireImage/Getty Images (with Bieber), Eugene Gologursky/WireImage/Getty Images (Mahone). 32: Jesse Grant/WireImage/Getty Images. 33: Michael Tran/FilmMagic/Getty (with mom), Jon Kopaloff/FilmMagic/Getty Images (Gomez). 34: Charley Gallay/Getty (with Minnie), Gareth Cattermole/Getty Images (Gomez). 35: Matt Carr/Getty Images. 36: Frazer Harrison/Getty Images. 37: Kevin Kolczynski/Universal Orlando Resort via Getty Images (arms out), Bryan Bedder/Getty Images for Nickelodeon (on stage). 38–39: Kevork Djansezian/Getty Images. 38: Matthew Peyton/Getty Images for Nickelodeon (all). 39: Matthew Peyton/Getty Images for Nickelodeon (all). 40: Virginia Sherwood/NBC/NBCU Photo Bank via Getty Images. 41: C Flanigan/WireImage/Getty Images. 42: George Pimentel/WireImage/Getty Images. 43: Jason Squires/WireImage. 44–45: James Devaney/WireImage/Getty Images. 45: Michael Caulfield/WireImage/Getty Images (with dancers), Kevin Mazur/WireImage/Getty Images (in purple). 46: Rob Kim/Getty Images. 47: ChinaFotoPress/ChinaFotoPress via Getty Images. 48: Shareif Ziyadat/FilmMagic/Getty Images. 49: Kevin Winter/Getty Images. 50–51: Photo by C Brandon/Redferns/Getty Images. 50: Paul Hawthorne/Getty Images. 52–53: Mike Marsland/WireImage/Getty Images. 53: Gabriel Olsen/FilmMagic/Getty Images (blue shirt), Steven Lawton/Getty Images (blazer). 54: Chris Polk/FilmMagic/Getty Images. 55: Jesse Grant/Getty Images for EMI Music. 56–57: Martin Philbey/Redferns/Getty Images. 56: Kristian Dowling/Getty Images. 58: John Gurzinski/Getty Images (president dress), Mike Marsland/WireImage/Getty Images (gold dress). 59: David Aguilera/BuzzFoto/FilmMagic/Getty Images. 60: Frederick M. Brown/Getty Images (button down), Ethan Miller/Getty Images (blue background). 61: Larry Busacca/Getty Images For The Recording Academy. 62–63 Ollie Millington/Redferns via Getty Images (all). 64–65: Ray Mickshaw/Fox via Getty Images (all). 66: Rachel Murray/WireImage/Getty Images. 67: Larry Busacca/Getty Images (with Big Time Rush), Alberto E. Rodriguez/Getty Images for KCA (Crow). 68: Steve Granitz/WireImage/Getty Images (abs), Jon Kopaloff/FilmMagic/Getty Images (thumbs up). 69: Adam Taylor/NBC/NBCU Photo Bank via Getty Images (hand in pocket), Chris Polk/FilmMagic/Getty Images (growl). 70–71: Michael Buckner/Getty Images for Lionsgate. 70: Kevork Djansezian/WireImage/Getty Images (award), Eamonn McCormack/WireImage/Getty Images (head). 72: Steve Granitz/WireImage/Getty Images (thumbs up), Gerardo Mora/Getty Images for Disney (blazer). 73: George Pimentel/WireImage/Getty Images. 74: Kevin Mazur/WireImage/Getty Images. 75: Jason Merritt/Getty Images for DCP (hands on hips), Dave Hogan/Getty Images (peace sign). 76–77: Kevin Mazur/WireImage/Getty Images. 76: Michael Buckner/Getty Images For (in black), D Dipasupil/FilmMagic/Getty Images (in red). 78: Jon Furniss/WireImage/Getty Images (crew neck), Jeff Kravitz/KCA2010/Getty Images (v neck). 79: Gareth Cattermole/Getty Images (balloons), Steve Granitz/WireImage/Getty Images (tie). 80–81: Neilson Barnard/Getty Images for Nickelodeon (all). 82–83: Press Association via AP Images. 84: Toby Zerna/Newspix/Getty Images (One Direction), Mike Marsland/WireImage/Getty Images (Malik). 85–86: Mike Marsland/WireImage/Getty Images (all). 87: Kevin Winter/Getty Images. 88: Paul Bergen/Redferns/Getty Images. 89: Christie Goodwin/Redferns/Getty Images. 90: Jo Hale/Getty Images. 91: Dan MacMedan/WireImage/Getty Images. 92: John Shearer/WireImage/Getty Images (hands to chest), Jon Kopaloff/FilmMagic/Getty Images (hand on hip). 93: Lester Cohen/WireImage/Getty Images. 94: Steve Thorne/Redferns via Getty Images. 95: Caitlin Mogridge/Redferns via Getty Images. 96–97: Joseph Okpako/Getty Images. 96: Vittorio Zunino Celotto/Getty Images. 97: Joseph Okpako/Getty Images. 98: Dave Hogan/Getty Images. 99: Ian Gavan/Getty Images. 100–101: Ian Gavan/Getty Images for MTV. 101: Dave Hogan/Getty Images. 102: Serge Thomann/WireImage/Getty Images (with family), Gaye Gerard/WireImage/Getty Images (Hemsworth). 103: Vera Anderson/WireImage/Getty Images. 104–105: Toby Canham/Getty Images. 104: Paul Drinkwater/NBC/NBCU Photo Bank via Getty Images. 106: Matt Roberts/Getty Images for Foot Locker/Pastry. 107: Neilson Barnard/WireImage/Getty Images (black shirt), Don Arnold/WireImage/Getty Images (white shirt). 108–109: Kevin Winter/Getty Images (all). 110: Michael Kovac/WireImage/Getty Images (Holt), David Livingston/Getty Images (Boldman, Sunshine), Taylor Hill/Getty Images (Mendler). 111: Jason LaVeris/FilmMagic/Getty Images (Cosgrove), Alberto E. Rodriguez/Getty Images (Austin), Gary Gershoff/WireImage/Getty Images (Lovato), Cindy Ord/Getty Images (Ryan). 112: Kevin Mazur/WireImage/Getty Images (Jackson), Stephen Lovekin/Getty Images (Madonna), Steve Mack/FilmMagic/Getty Images (Jay-Z). 113: Jeffrey Mayer/WireImage/Getty Images (Timberlake), Jim Spellman/WireImage/Getty Images (Beyonce), Michael Loccisano/Getty Images for Usher's New Look Foundation (Usher). 114: Gabriel Olsen/FilmMagic/Getty Images (Ne-yo), C Flanigan/FilmMagic/Getty Images (Drake), Bill McCay/WireImage/Getty Images (Sheeran). 115: Phil Dent/Redferns/Getty Images (Jackson), James Devaney/WireImage/Getty Images (Bieber), Jon Kopaloff/FilmMagic/Getty Images (Maslow). 116: Kevin Mazur/WireImage/Getty Images (Mahone), Michael Kovac/WireImage/Getty Images (Simpson), Slaven Vlasic/Getty Images (Maynard), Jason Merritt/Getty Images (Bieber), Dimitrios Kambouris/Getty Images (Perry). 117: C Flanigan/WireImage/Getty Images (Schmidt), Josiah Kamau/BuzzFoto/FilmMagic/Getty Images (Lady Gaga), Ben Pruchnie/Getty Images for Westfield (Payne), Stephen Lovekin/Getty Images (Lerman), Albert L. Ortega/Getty Images (Lautner). 119: Caroline McCredie/Getty Images (Bieber), Paul Drinkwater/NBC/NBCU Photo Bank via Getty Images (Minaj). 120: Nick Rood/Young Hollywood/Getty Images (Cruikshank), Imeh Akpanudosen/Getty Images (Gomez), David Livingston/Getty Images (Hemsworth), Jon Kopaloff/FilmMagic/Getty Images (Swift). 121: Mary Clavering/Young Hollywood/Getty Images (Ne-yo), Rachel Murray/Getty Images (Crow), Steve Granitz/WireImage/Getty Images (Drake), Christopher Polk/KCA2012/Getty Images for KCA (Lautner). 122: David Livingston/Getty Images (Fegan), Imeh Akpanudosen/Getty Images (Maslow), Jason Merritt/Getty Images for John Varvatos (Palmer). 123: Slaven Vlasic/Getty Images (Simpson), Robin Marchant/Getty Images (Grande), Jon Kopaloff/FilmMagic/Getty Images (Kagasoff), Frazer Harrison/Getty Images for PCA (Crow). 124: Kevin Mazur/WireImage/Getty Images (One Direction), KAZUHIRO NOGI/AFP/Getty Images (Lady Gaga), Kevin Mazur/WireImage/Getty Images (Bieber), Caitlin Mogridge/Redferns via Getty Images (Maynard). 125: Kevin Winter/Getty Images (Perry), Dave J Hogan/Getty Images (Swift), Jeff Kravitz/FilmMagic/Getty Images (Minaj), Kevin Mazur/WireImage/Getty Images (Lovato). 126: David Livingston/Getty Images (Simpson), Jeff Vespa/WireImage/Getty Images (Perry), David Caird/Newspix via Getty Images (Bieber). 127: Danny Martindale/Getty Images (Minaj), Josiah Kamau/BuzzFoto/FilmMagic/Getty Images (Lady Gaga), Henry S. Dziekan III/FilmMagic/Getty Images (Schmidt), Michael Buckner/Getty Images for AIF (Hemsworth). Giant pull-out photo of Taylor Swift: Christopher Polk/Getty Images for Clear Channel; giant pull-out photo of Cody Simpson: Brad Barket/Getty Images; giant pull-out photo of Justin Bieber: Jason Merritt/Getty Images; giant pull-out photos of One Direction: Kevin Kane/Getty Images for Jingle Ball 2012.